FIREMAN
ON THE RUN

FIREMAN
ON THE RUN

TERRY LANE

BROWN
DOG
BOOKS

Published under licence by Brown Dog Books and The Self-Publishing Partnership, 7 Green Park Station, Bath BA1 1JB

www.selfpublishingpartnership.co.uk

ISBN printed book: 978-1-78545-140-9
ISBN e-book: 978-1-78545-141-6

Cover design by Kevin Rylands
Internal design by Andrew Easton
Front cover illustration by Eddie Smith

Printed and bound by CPI Group (UK) Ltd, Croydon CR0 4YY

I dedicate this book to my two
granddaughters, Jessica and Poppy.
An insight into the strange world of your
granddad - fireman and marathon runner.
I wrote this book while training to run the
London Marathon.
Thank you for the joy and happiness you have
both given to Nanny and me.
Also a big thank-you to my wonderful wife Eve,
our two children Kev and Julie for their support
in both the training and the Fire Service.

*This book is based on a 16-week training
programme to run the London Marathon.
Each chapter is one week of training.*

CHAPTER 1

SIXTEEN WEEKS TO GO

Week 1, Day 1: New Year's Eve, and it says 45 minutes' run/walk

I think I can handle that quite easily, probably won't bother with the walk side of it. After all, I have many half-marathons and even one full marathon under my belt.

Ok, it may be two years or so since I have done any serious running since an injury at work.

I remember it well. I was taking a physical training session in the morning, stressing how important it is to do a good warm-up to prevent injury. As usual, I spoke too soon and felt this terrific pain in my back. Here I was, the Watch physical training instructor, being helped home by a couple of beer-swilling, heavy-smoking firemen telling me how this physical training lark is bad for you. Perhaps they may have a point.

Well, after 48 hours of lying on the floor of the lounge, unable to do anything except feel sorry for myself and consider smoking again, and perhaps even a few extra pints wouldn't hurt, I was taken to hospital.

The ambulance arrived to pick me up; it just had to be one of the very few ambulance drivers that I knew.

"I thought you firemen were supposed to be fit; it's all this physical training you do. It's bad for you, you know."

I was admitted to an orthopaedic ward in the local General Hospital where I spent 3 weeks with a further two weeks in the Neurological Unit.

After various tests, myelograms and x-rays, they decide I needed to have two discs removed, a laminectomy. Due to the seriousness of nerves being trapped around the discs they had to transfer me to a neuro ward for a neurosurgeon to do the operation.

When I first met the surgeon, he told me that it would be a major operation, and if anything should go wrong I could end up spending the rest of my life in a wheelchair. "Oh, you will never go back to the Fire Service," he said as he left.

Well, the operation was a success, and after seven days flat on my back, they got me up to start the long process of getting fit again. I started off with hydrotherapy three times a week; and then gentle physiotherapy.

I was determined to prove the surgeon wrong and get back to work. With the help of some very good physios, extra physiotherapy, and kicks up the backside from Eve whenever I felt sorry for myself, I returned to work as a fireman after 9 months off sick.

New Year's Eve: 45-minute walk/run

I drove to Southampton Common and began running. After 2 minutes my chest is burning, legs aching. I'm convinced that I must be mad. I'm a stone overweight, have high blood pressure, had a laminectomy and collapsed lung, and hadn't run for two years.

Here's me thinking I can just carry on as if it was yesterday.

I soon found my first excuse for a walk: it came in the form of a black shadow leaping at me from the bushes, a very large Dobermann minus its owner. My first thought was to break into some fartlek training, but this doesn't start until week five; so I decided to walk.

I placed my hands on my hips and spat, hoping anyone watching would think that I had stopped purely because of the dog. Little did they know a squirrel would have been a good enough excuse. The dog's owner appeared, whistled and the dog changed direction and bounded off after its owner.

I was walking when I saw another runner approaching, so I decided to start running again. As he drew level I lifted my arm to glance at my watch and to say, "bloody dogs", when I remembered the strap on my watch had broken six months previously and it was in my pocket. I don't suppose he noticed…..

I thought I would have another walk now: I must have been running for 25 minutes or so. What a disappointment, only 8 minutes. I managed to plod on with quite a few walks and a lot less runs for the 45 minutes.

I got back to the car: getting in was no problem, getting out was where the fun started. I didn't think it was possible for the legs to seize up quite so quickly. How was I going to get out of the car while the neighbours looked on, thinking here comes that nutter again trying to make a comeback.

Well, I gritted my teeth, climbed out of the car, fell up onto the kerb and nearly went head first through the front door.

After soaking in a hot bath before going out to celebrate the New Year, I thought I would have a look to see what is in store for New Year's Day. 26 minutes' continuous jog.

I decide to cut down on the beer tonight, and get up early and do the 26 minutes.

Day 2: New Year's Day 26-minute jog

I wake up at 11.15 am with a real hangover after a gallon of best bitter, 20 minutes of "Auld Lang Syne", various congers and a good rendition of "When the Saints" to Eve saying, "Are you coming up the Common with the dogs, or staying in bed all day?"

I eventually decide to go to the Common. I swing my legs out of bed; they feel as if they have been hit with a plank of wood, as stiff as a corporal on his wedding night. I manage to hobble and limp down the stairs, only to find my training booklet waiting for me on the table. I have always said that Eve has a sick sense of humour.

20 minutes of continuous jog, some hope. After some considerable thought and a kick up the backside by Eve, she – sorry, I should say we – decide that Eve will drive to the Common with the dogs and I would run.

After helping put the dogs into the car, I decide to do some stretching and try and get the legs working again. This is also to try and gain a bit more time, allowing Eve to get further around her marathon circuit of the Common. If I can time it right I should meet Eve just as she is returning to the car.

I leave home at a very steady, and I do mean steady, pace for the 1.5 miles to the Common. A quick fumble in my pocket for the watch, I must get a new strap, 10 minutes gone, right on target. Another mile to the car should take me nicely up to the required 20 minutes. Another fumble in the pocket, fifteen minutes gone. Where the devil is Eve and the dogs.

I decide to continue running in the direction I think Eve

will come from, 18 minutes gone, lungs really burning, legs feel like lead weights. If I could find the dogs I might be able to fall over them and lie down for an hour or two.

I think I must have had a bad pint or six last night to make me feel like this. 19 minutes gone, oh well, only one minute left.

There in the distance are Eve and the dogs, I'll carry on jogging towards them for one minute and the 20 is complete and wait for them to come to me.

No such luck, they carried on a parallel course, leaving me to hobble after them. A further 30 minutes of walking and cursing before we all returned to the car. Where Eve says, "We should do this more often."

Back indoors and a long-awaited sit-down to listen to Radio Solent to hear the Saints match up at Sunderland.

After sitting for about half an hour, I realise that no one else, and I mean Eve, is going to make a cup of tea and I had better make the effort. What a mistake, I can't move from the waist down. I was seized up.

After some rubbing, cursing and sheer guts, I manage to get mobile and soak in a hot bath.

Back to work tomorrow, I hope we have an easy day. I have a quick look in the training programme to see what tomorrow will bring. 35-minute run/walk, swim or rest if stiff and tired. I'll make the choice in the morning.

By the way, Saints lost 1-0.

Day 3: 35-minute run/walk/swim or rest if stiff and tired

Woke up this morning feeling very fluey. I think I will opt for the rest day. That was until Eve reminded me that I was going to leave the car for her and walk to work. Oh well, I can treat the walk, about 1.5 miles, as training.

I leave home and it's blowing a gale. Never mind, good training I think, hoping that we will have a nice easy day.

08.59, Duty watch parade, the roll-call is taken and I'm detailed to drive the hydraulic platform, a machine designed for rescue purposes.

A quick cup of tea and then it's full kit for drill. You name it, we did it. Ladders up everywhere, hose run out around the yard, pretend salvage work; all this with legs that feel like lead and a nose like a tap.

Time for a tea break, and then physical training. It is pouring with rain and someone suggests that we go down the local park for a game of football. I decide to treat the football as 35 minutes of running and walking.

What an idiot, there must have been an inch of water everywhere. At one stage it looks as if I should have opted for the swim. I manage to keep going, mainly running for 45 minutes, even putting in a few sprints. 10 minutes in credit, I think.

Back to the station, time for a quick shower: 'quick' being the operative word because we are still on call. Then lunch.

What a mistake sitting down for an hour: come 2 o'clock I could hardly move. Luckily we have no calls during the afternoon. I decide to phone Eve and ask her to come and pick me up: well, it is pouring with rain after all.

Day 4: 20-minute continuous jog

Had a really rough night coughing and sneezing, so have decided to rest from training today and train on Friday instead.

I still had to go to work – walking, may I add, as Eve needed the car.

After the parade we are told that we will be doing a breathing apparatus drill, we are told to get into full kit and wait in the lecture room.

We are divided into two teams, one of four and the other three, me being in the 4-man crew.

Well, in the Fire Brigade, the first mention of teams, it's us and them; it's all stops out to be the best, to win or whatever.

We are told that there has been a fire in a disused garage that was under receivership, and Persons Reported, which means to us that somebody is trapped inside. My team is to go into the ground-floor building, on a right-hand search. The other team has been told to go on a left-hand search, whereby we should both meet approximately halfway round, and hopefully have searched the outside of the entire ground floor.

Our officer in charge is into video cameras, so he decided that he would video the drill to show our mistakes.

Well, he's either unfamiliar with the camera, or was so taken back with our search procedure, he forgot to turn the camera on.

We manage to find our dummy, hanging from the rafters, a supposed suicide.

This brought some memories flooding back to me of one of the times when we had a real job similar to this. I was riding BA (which means in the event of a fire my partner and I would be the first to go into the incident).

It was the early hours of the morning when we received a Persons Reported call to a business premises with living accommodation above.

The first BA crew had entered the building, and thought they could see somebody through the thick smoke coming down the stairs. They grabbed hold of him, when he started swinging they realised that the chap had hanged himself.

I was in the next crew of two to enter. My partner Dave was a new recruit, this was his first dead body, which was not helped by it being a hanging.

Our task was to get up the stairs and search the flat above. While doing this we found a doorway which led down to a basement. I don't mind admitting, I was a bit nervous going down there. I suppose he had murdered the rest of the family and then hanged himself: what were we going to find?

My first thought was to let the new recruit go first, purely for the experience: well, that was my excuse. I managed to stay in control and lead the way, trying to remember back to training school days some sixteen years previously, on dealing with fatal fires.

We needed to take note of which doors were open, which ones we had opened; were any bolted etc., also trying to reassure the poor young lad with me; thankfully, all we found was an empty basement.

The drill was very different. We had a good laugh as we could hear the other crew bumping into various objects, placed at the right height to catch you where it hurts most. Still, the drill was successfully completed.

A quick cup of tea before physical training. A good warm-up followed by 20 minutes of football. All this on a rest day. I thought, oh well, nights tomorrow and a 20-minute continuous jog.

Day 5: 20-minute continuous jog

Woke up this morning feeling a lot better and decided to go to the Utd Cup match. What a queue, I'll leave it today and go the beginning of next week.

I must be getting old: once upon a time I would have queued for hours. In fact, all night outside the ground in freezing conditions to get a ticket for the quarter-final game against Bradford City at Bradford.

At 2 o'clock in the morning there must have been 50-a-side playing football in the street. What a great atmosphere.

Oh well, put the running shoes on and do a few stretches, still feeling good. Perhaps I should do Sunday's 50-minute walk and run today.

Set the stopwatch and away. Quarter of a mile down the road the legs start aching, lungs burning; I think I'll stick to the 20 minutes. I fumble for the watch in my tracksuit trousers and get some very strange looks from the people at the bus stop.

Eight minutes gone, I know I have just completed a mile from the days when I used to have numerous measured landmarks: not bad, I thought, an 8-minute mile.

I run past The Dell, there's no queue: typical when I don't have my voucher or money with me.

Another jogger coming in the opposite direction:

stomach in, look at missing wristwatch, raise right hand and say hi as we pass. A quick glance over my shoulder, now safe to let the stomach out; I must do something about the size of me.

Totally mistimed this run, as I enter my road I see that I'm 1 minute and 30 seconds over time.

Straight into a hot bath: as I'm lying there, I think I should have done Sunday's run today as I'm on nights today and tomorrow and I don't normally feel like anything during the days, let alone a 35-minute and 50-minute walk and run on Saturday and Sunday.

Oh well, let's hope for a couple of quiet nights. Hopefully the weathermen may be wrong, and the gale-force winds they have forecast may miss us. It's not very nice up on a roof in the middle of the night in gale-force winds.

Day 6: 35-minute run/walk

Not a bad night at work, had about 4 hours' sleep: sounds bad, doesn't it? 4 hours' sleep at work. Perhaps I should explain, we work two days between 9 am and 6 pm, then two nights from 6 pm to 9 am. When on nights we are allowed to sleep between midnight and 7 am, but must remain immediately available for any call. I'm afraid I never sleep well when you know that any second the alarm bells may go off and you have to be on the road within 30 seconds.

About 2.30 in the morning the police ring up to ask if we could remove some handcuffs from a man who just happened to turn up at the police station wearing handcuffs. They didn't have a key to fit. Five minutes of sawing through a rivet and he was free. We never did find out why he was wearing them.

The gale-force winds they were predicting seemed to be getting nearer, and at 5.30 am we get a call to an automatic fire alarm set off by the wind.

Oh well, no point going back to bed. I help to cook the breakfast, clear up, and the next thing it's 9 am, off duty, and I change into my running gear.

Feel quite good this morning so decide to run home the long way, and to do Sunday's run on Saturday and Saturday's run on Sunday. I can never do things normally. Off I go, 50 minutes' walk/run.

I must start planning the routes better. I decided to run along a footpath which was ankle-deep in mud up to the sports centre, all grass. I wish I had studs or spikes that may have enabled me to stay on my feet.

Quick fumble for the watch, 16 minutes gone and I'm still feeling pretty good, although I had to do a few forced walks, or should I say paddles. Back onto the road and into the Common then home.

A nice soak, and a dangerous sleep in the bath. A spot of lunch, then off to The Dell to see Saints v Ipswich in the third round of the FA Cup.

It's going to be a rush, I'm due back on nights at 18.00. A good result for Saints, 3-2 win and into the hat for tomorrow's 4th-round draw.

17.59 Duty Watch Parade. BA on the back of the Water Tender tonight, a nice change from driving.

Poor old Dave, a 6ft 4in Scot, and only just out of training school, let it slip that he used to be a trainspotter. After all the usual noises and jokes, we presented him with a place mat with a picture of a child's train. He had to use this at every meal.

During the evening we got a couple of calls, one to people trapped in a lift, and the other to a smell of burning at the General Hospital.

The second call took a bit of time to trace as we were getting reports from every floor level of a smell of burning. We eventually traced it to the basement where an electrical coil had burnt out.

Back to the station, a quick cup of tea, wash and chamois both appliances and off to bed. Just one call during the night to a private hospital: this turned out to be a false alarm.

CHAPTER 2

FIFTEEN WEEKS TO GO

Week 2, Day 1: 50-minute run/walk

I leave work at 09.00 and arrive home at 10 past. Quick change and off to church with Eve. Luckily it was a good, lively sermon all about the meaning of Epiphany. I decided to leave the run until late-afternoon to give me a chance for an hour's sleep after lunch.

Watched the match on BBC1, then a good warm-up, and off on a 35-minute run/walk. If you remember I did Sunday's run on Saturday, and now I'm doing Saturday's run on Sunday (should it be this complicated?).

Felt quite good again today, not very much walking and not too many aches and pains. After the first week things are coming along nicely. A day off training tomorrow and I'm going birdwatching with a friend of mine. I've never done this before and quite looking forward to it.

A couple of pints in front of the telly tonight, followed by an early night to catch up on lost sleep.

Day 2: Day off

What a lovely sleep, must be getting used to our new orthopaedic bed: at first it was as though we were sleeping on concrete, now it's more like tarmac (just a little bit of give).

Eve's done me a nice packed lunch. After a few jokes about making sure it's only the feathered sort I look at, I leave home to pick up Roger, a good friend who has decided that I need educating in the finer things of life.

Our first port of call is the Lower Test, where there is a hide; you can sit and look at the various species across the marshes without them seeing you.

As we enter the hide I'm most impressed: there's a long bench seat with a shelf in front to rest the compulsory bird books and a small porthole window to look out with binoculars or telescope, or in most cases both.

We are told by two mature gentlemen sitting in the hide that "there's not a lot about". I look across the marshes to the houses on the other side and wonder if they realise that they can be spied on with these powerful binoculars and telescopes. And what sort of birds were they referring to when they said there's not a lot about?

Roger decided we may get on better down at Calshot: there are no hides there or houses.

The wind is blowing hard off the sea, so it's on with the cap and wellie boots; binoculars around my neck and off we trek for one of the most relaxing days that I can remember.

Roger is pointing out various species of gull. I thought they were all seagulls and that was that; how wrong you can be. We must have walked a total of 5 or 6 miles on a circular route: over a period of about 5 hours, we had seen and heard various species.

The highlight for me was to see several curlews in flight and feeding in the marshes. Back to the car just before a downpour. My luck must be changing.

Day 3: 20-minute continuous run

A rough day today, wind blowing and pouring with rain. Decide to do a run about lunchtime. I have an appointment with Bob Donovan my 'Alexander Technique' teacher. After my back operation I had still been getting pains in my legs that orthodox medicine no longer helps. I was referred to Bob after a course of acupuncture by the doctor.

The Alexander Technique is basically relieving the body of stress through various movements which, in time, gets the body to work as one, as opposed to various muscles working with or against each other.

After a 45-minute session, I feel that I could run a marathon. Apparently a lot of back problems are caused by bad posture, another thing that the Alexander Technique helps to improve.

Lunchtime and it's still pouring with rain and blowing a gale. I decide to drop Julie, my daughter, at college, then park at the Common and do my 20 minutes.

Feeling really good again today, the rest yesterday seems to have paid off. I approach Cemetery Lake which has overflowed right across the path; I have to pick my way between ducks and swans now swimming on the path.

I remember my last conflict with a swan, it was 2 o'clock in the morning; I was part of a Fire Brigade team taking part in a canoe race between Bristol Docks and Windsor. We had a crew of 8 paddlers plus support vehicles: their task was to feed and look after us. We had planned our changeover points in advance, having allowed for access, the flow of water etc. It usually worked out that each pair did 5 to 6 miles in one stint; they then had a rest while another pair took over.

Phil and I had taken over somewhere near Newbury when we came across a load of swans with their young swimming in front of us. We were told during training that if a swan should attack us, to pull over to the side and let them pass. Well, this is all very well in training on a lake or pond. But on a fast-flowing river in the middle of the night, it's a different matter.

One of the swans broke away from the group and swam towards us hissing and spitting. We slowed down for a bit which seemed to work for a minute or two. Then the swan turned again and started running along the water with its neck stretched out and flapping its wings. I was in the front of the canoe: as the swan leapt at us, we both leant to our left, and over we went into the Kennet and Avon Canal.

We had to swim to the bank dragging the upturned canoe with us. We decided to climb out onto the bank and empty the water out of the canoe. This might sound very flash, but at 2 am when you are freezing cold and soaking wet, it's not quite so simple.

After about 10 minutes, struggling up this steep, slippery bank with the canoe, we decide to run with the canoe on our shoulders until we were past the swans.

I'm convinced those swans wanted to join in the race: it must have been about 2 miles before we passed them and were able to get back into the water.

So here I am in the middle of the Common, talking to the swans as if they are dogs: "There's a good boy, then."

I managed to continue with the run with an occasional glance over the shoulder to check that the swans aren't chasing me.

The visibility is down to about 20 yards with the torrential rain: my tracksuit trousers are feeling really heavy with the soaking, I push on to the car. Once back inside I fish around for the watch (I must get a new strap) and I'm surprised to see that I was running for 22 minutes.

Home to a nice hot bath, some abuse from my son Kev, who thinks I'm mad at my age to start running again, and into some nice dry clothes.

Day 4: 40-minute run/walk

Feeling tired this morning, but legs feel ok. I decide to go on one of my routes of about 5 miles which I can cut short if I run out of time. Weather a lot better today: the sun is actually trying to shine, but quite a strong wind blowing.

The first look at the watch, 26 minutes gone and chest feeling good, I seem to have got rid of that burning feeling. Legs feeling really heavy but manage to plod on with only two small walks.

A quick look at watch: 38 minutes gone and still a mile from home. I keep on running, 46 minutes; the credit side must be really building up.

A visit to the doctor this afternoon for a check-up: he said he's very pleased with me, and off I go to the chemist to get my prescription. The lady assistant looks at the prescription and says that there is no charge for these; a cold shiver goes down my spine as I think that these pills must be the only thing keeping me alive.

"Are you sure?" I ask. "Yes, they are pills, aren't they?" she says. "Yes," I say, "they are not liquid." She looks at me as if I'm stupid. "No. The Pill," she says, looking at the name on the front of the prescription, stating Mr. Lane. "I didn't know they did them for men."

I then realised that she was referring to the 'Birth Pill'

which apparently was very similar in name to my tablets. I was quite pleased to pay the £3.05.

Back on duty tomorrow and due for a 20-minute continuous jog; hopefully I can include this in the PT session, or perhaps I might change and have a 20-minute swim. Every Thursday we have the use of a swimming pool for an hour at the local girls' school.

Day 5: 20-minute continuous jog

Back on days today, and driving the hydraulic platform. I've been asked if I could help out on a local course today and tomorrow, training men as operators for the HP.

What normally happens is that when the HP is sent out on a call, it goes with two firemen, one being the driver/operator whose job is to get the HP to the incident, contact the officer in charge and site the platform, for whatever task is required.

Once it's in position, and the cage in which the firemen are standing is in a safe position in the air, the controls are handed over to a cage operator. The driver operator, who is still at ground level, has still got overall control if needed.

The course is purely for training cage operators and consists of one hour in the classroom, then plenty of practical operating. Which means, in my case, standing at the base and constantly looking up and being ready to take over control should the need arise.

As you can imagine, by the end of the day, I have a really terrible neck ache.

Quite recently another of these courses was being run, and as part of the practical training, we had permission to use the local hospital. We would practise going up and down the building trying to stay as close to the windows as possible: this would be good training should we ever have to carry out rescues from the windows.

Well, permission was given by the hospital, but due to some oversight the wards were not told. This led to a lady on the cardiac ward being given the fright of her life when she saw the head and shoulders of three grinning firemen appearing at the window on the third floor.

We have stopped using the site now.

11.15 and time to go swimming. I decide that if I can get 20 minutes swimming in I will treat this as my training for today.

No calls and a good swim in which I manage to swim 20 lengths in 20 minutes. Although we are in the water we must still be immediately available: this means leaving one man on the fire engine listening to the radio and in contact with our control. You can imagine the panic when we get a call.

I was in the shower at the station once when we got a call to an old people's home. I had just shampooed my hair when we had a shout. I had some very strange looks from the residents as I stood there with soap bubbles falling from under my helmet.

Day 6: Rest day

Today should be a rest day in preparation for two hard days of training on Saturday and Sunday. I decide to incorporate our football session into a 40-minute run/walk, and then on Saturday, the first of my two nights, to do Sunday's 1-hour walk/run.

Back to Friday, and we play a good 40 minutes of football in really heavy, muddy conditions. I manage to keep moving and so treat this as my training session.

We had a call this morning right on changeover (this meant we had a mixture of night shift and day shift) to a man trapped under a lorry. We arrived after great difficulty getting through the rush hour traffic, to find a man under an articulated lorry. Although seriously injured, he was not trapped, so it was a case of helping the ambulance men and police to get him out and into the ambulance.

Apparently the lorry was turning left and didn't see the cyclist on his left, who was dragged under the lorry and then 20 yards along the road.

Finished off the HP course during the afternoon: the legs are feeling really tired. It must have been all the mud. A nice quiet evening in front of the telly with a can of beer.

Day 7: 40-minute run/walk

Woke up this morning with legs feeling really heavy. Going to do Sunday's 1-hour run/walk today, as I had done Saturday's on Friday. This really is getting complicated. Change into my running gear and do a good warm-up. I make sure that I have got a 10p piece in case I need to phone Eve to come and pick me up.

Legs feeling heavy, breathing quite good. It says in the training guide to cut down on the walking; so decide to try and run for 30 minutes without walking around the Common.

The Common looks beautiful today with the sun shining, then out into the street behind the university for a long, uphill climb.

A quick glance at my watch, 38 minutes done and feeling pretty good but decide to head for home and get back in the allocated time.

Back into the Common, two miles from home and 50 minutes done with just one short walk. I get home feeling really pleased with myself. 1 hour 6 minutes with only one short walk.

A long soak in the bath, check the radio so that I can listen to the Saints game and settle down for an easy afternoon before going on nights. What a good result: Saints won 4-3 away to Luton. Off to work, and apart from a standby call at 1 o'clock a quiet night.

CHAPTER 3

FOURTEEN WEEKS TO GO

Day 1: One hour of running/walking

Arrive home from work just after 9 am, happy in the knowledge that I can have a rest because I did Sunday's run on Saturday.

Off to church with Eve, then home to help get Sunday lunch ready. An afternoon in front of the telly to watch the Big Match: Everton v Manchester City. I'm afraid I don't see much of it as I fall asleep; Eve woke me at 4.30 to say that I had better start getting ready for work.

I decide to give a friend of mine a ring first; he lives in Wareham, Dorset. I met Fred in the Wessex Neurological Centre when I was having an operation on my back. He was such a calming influence, and kept me in stitches (excuse the pun).

I remember one day a chap had been brought into the ward; he was put in the bed opposite Fred and me. We all got talking on the subject of coloured doctors; Fred was going on about one who looked like a witch doctor who probably dances around the ward when we are all asleep.

He made some unprintable remarks, and we left it at that. When visiting time arrived, a very attractive black woman walked into the ward and sat opposite us. Yes, it was this chap's wife. Fred just waved, winked at me and pretended to go to sleep.

17.59 Duty watch parade, I'm detailed to drive the hydraulic platform, another quiet night. Things seem really quiet lately: still, I'm not complaining.

Day 2: Rest day

I decide to do Tuesday's 25-minute continuous run today. I set off feeling tired with really heavy legs. I get a really tight feeling in my right calf and shin but manage to plod on. This seems like one of the worst runs in a long time, although I do manage to finish.

I soak in a hot bath feeling pretty cheesed off.

Eve, who works part-time for an insurance company, is working overtime today and will not be home until 3.30 pm, so I decide to have a day of hoovering and cooking. I enjoy the cooking side. It's a case of having to learn to cook in my job. Although we have a cook on days, weekends and nights we have to do our own meals, so we take it in turns to cook.

Some of the chaps are very good, but I'm afraid not all. It's quite harrowing for a new recruit to come onto a Watch and to be told to cook a roast for ten. Some cope well, mainly the married men, but others really struggle.

We have one young lad who cooks quite well, but just can't crack eggs into the frying pan in the morning for breakfast without breaking them. He takes so much stick over these eggs that it really worries him.

One morning he managed 8 out of 8 whole eggs and was really pleased with himself. We were just about to eat our breakfast when we got a shout, arriving back after 45 minutes. All the eggs were dried up like leather; I thought he was going to cry.

Day 3: 25-minute continuous jog

I was hoping to do Wednesday's training today because I'm going birdwatching again tomorrow during the day, then to the Saints v Manchester Utd game in the evening; but I got out of bed in the night to go to the loo and felt this sharp pain in my back. It's not too bad in the morning, but still a bit sore.

Had an appointment with Bob Donovan this morning and he manages to make me feel pretty good; I decide not to run today, but to borrow Kev's bike and to do an hour of cycling instead.

We have some good cycle tracks in Southampton, so I set off on one heading towards Eling. It's a beautiful morning with the sun shining, but with a cold wind blowing. I'd forgotten how hard saddles on racing bikes are; I spend quite a bit of time riding standing up instead of sitting down.

It has been three years since I was into serious cycle training, ready to take part in a sponsored tandem ride with the rest of red watch between John o' Groats and Land's End.

It was initially my idea, and I organised all the practicalities such as two tandems, fuel for the support vehicles, food was being donated by Little Chef restaurants; but I had to drop out at the last minute due to the back injury and being in hospital.

The local radio station, Radio Solent, followed the ride with daily updates and progress reports. It was very frustrating lying flat on my back listening to the daily radio bulletin. The lads made it ok and we raised over £2000 for the Fire Brigade Benevolent Fund.

I promised myself that one day I'll attempt the ride but make sure that I have a soft saddle.

After the hour's ride I decide to try and rest my back as much as possible today, hoping that tomorrow I'll be back to normal.

Day 4: 40-minute run/walk

The back is feeling a lot better today so pick Roger up for my second time of birdwatching. We decide to go to Pennington Marshes and Keyhaven. We walk along the front with binoculars around our necks; we meet a gentleman who looks like an old sea dog, including the white beard.

After an excited conversation between this gent and Roger, which was completely over my head, I'm informed that quite a rare bird to these shores has been seen on the Marshes.

Roger explains that a little egret has been seen, and with a bit of luck we may get a sighting.

We set off along the sea wall following signs for the Solent Way: a cold wind is blowing off the sea, but it is still quite pleasant.

I make a mental note that this is an ideal place for a run, and is a circular route of six miles.

We stop after about an hour for a cup of tea from the flasks, and a much-needed sit-down. All of a sudden I hear a choking sound and as I run to Roger's aid, he's pointing and shouting to look across the Marshes.

I do but all I can see is a white bird walking across the marsh. I turn back to Roger and he's now setting up his telescope with one hand and looking through his binoculars with the other, shouting, "That's it, the little egret!"

I must admit that once I take note of what he's saying, I become quite excited. Here's me out for only the second time, seeing a bird that quite a few experienced birdwatchers have never seen.

We carry on walking after all the excitement and meet

other birdwatchers. They all ask, "Is there much about?", for me to quickly say only a little egret.

We finished our circular walk in about 4 hours and drive back to Southampton.

It's off to The Dell tonight for the quarter-final of the Rumbelows Cup. It's a total sell-out to see Saints draw 1-1 in a really exciting Cup match.

As I walk home from the match I feel a bit guilty that I haven't done a training run today. I tell myself I'll make up for it tomorrow.

Day 5: 25-minute run

I wake up this morning to the news that America and her allies have attacked Kuwait and Iraq. I hope this will be over soon, and feel for the families of the men and women who are out in the Gulf.

I drop Julie at college, and then do the catering for work. I'm the Watch Caterer, and it's my job to buy the food for the tour of duty. The lads all pay a certain amount of money each tour and it's my job to buy the lunches, suppers and breakfast, as well as tea and coffee. The Fire Brigade pay me three hours' overtime a tour for doing this.

As you can imagine, the mess manager takes a bit of stick over the menus etc. but after doing the job for 12 years I've heard all the cracks and can normally come up with a good answer.

After the shopping it's into running kit and off into the sunshine. I feel a bit heavy in the legs, but that seems to ease off as I get going. I notice that I'm running at a faster pace than normal and run for 40 minutes, that's 15 minutes over.

I spend the afternoon doing bits and pieces around the house, also listening to the radio for reports on the Gulf.

Back to work tomorrow and a rest day in the training schedule.

Day 6: Rest day

Back to work today and I'm detailed to drive the Water Tender Ladder. This appliance is designed for fire-fighting, also dealing with road traffic accidents. We also carry a 50-ft ladder.

We spend the morning on the drill yard practising for leading fireman drills. These are for men wishing to take the practical exam to gain the rank of leading fireman.

They have to take charge of a drill session, and to correct any mistakes that they notice. A few years ago, the crew were allowed to make as many mistakes as they liked. You used to get chaps putting their helmets on back to front, cigarettes hanging out of their mouths, hiding in lockers etc.

The poor candidate taking the exam was supposed to notice all these things, and then put them right. Then the powers that be decided that enough natural mistakes were being made, and therefore stopped all the deliberate ones.

After lunch we do an hour of cleaning and standard tests. Then it's down to the local park for a warm-up and a game of football. 30 minutes of running and kicking in the thick mud, I feel quite knackered.

We spend the evening visiting both sets of parents, and then a nice early night so that I can be up early to do Saturday's training before work.

Day 7: 45-minute run/walk

I stagger out of bed at 6.30 am and get ready for a run. I decide I will take a long route to work, and keep going for 45 minutes. I set off feeling very heavy in the legs, heading towards the Common. As I reach my first-mile marker I look at the watch, 8 minutes done, through the Common and a long, uphill stretch, out onto the road, feeling a bit looser now, then into the sports centre for about a mile then back onto the road.

Check my watch and 33 minutes gone. Now through some woods and along a wooden walkway, across a small stream, back on the road, up a steep hill and into the station. Exactly 45 minutes and no walking.

A nice hot shower, then on parade for 08.59 where I'm detailed to drive the HP. I'm asked if I would do the cooking today so that the fireman who should have been the cook could take part in drills, as he is still a probationer.

I spend the first two hours making a turkey curry and a cheesecake.

After the 11 am tea break it's down to the park for a game of football. I volunteer to stay on the appliance and listen to the radio in case we get a call; the old legs are really aching.

Back to the station and I manage to get through the gates first time. The Hydraulic Platform is 36ft long and it's very difficult getting through the gates without having to back up. I went through a spell where every time I had to back up, causing a laugh with the rest of the Watch.

An hour left to cook the rice and finish off the curry. A success, 10 empty plates and a lot of sweaty foreheads.

After lunch I'm put into the workshop to repair hose. I

really wish I had brought my radio so that I could listen to the Saints match at home to Nottingham Forest.

I have to wait until I get home to hear the score, a 1-1 draw.

CHAPTER 4

THIRTEEN WEEKS TO GO

Day 1: One and a half to one and three-quarters hours' run/walk

I decided to do the run mid-morning so that I can get back for Sunday lunch, then have my legs up while watching the match on the box.

I set off on a ten-mile circular course, with my 10p piece in my pocket, in case I need to phone home.

The first four miles is all slightly uphill and I feel very tired when I reach that stage. I carry on past all the big houses of Chilworth; at one stage I have to jump out of the way as a BMW comes out of one of the drives and straight across the pavement.

During the run I think of all the lads out in the Gulf and realise how lucky I am to be able to run in freedom like this.

I'm now on a volunteer list to be called out at any time to help with casualty handling, if and when they are brought into Eastleigh Airport en route to various hospitals in the south.

I keep on running and check my watch, I really must get a strap, 50 minutes done. I now enter the Plantation to shouts and cheers, and cries of "Well done, mate, you're doing well." I take a glance over my shoulder to realise that I have got myself caught up in a cross-country race; I'm leading by about 50 yards.

I'm tempted to run for the line and claim first prize; being the sportsman that I am, I carry on along the track, trying to convince a race marshal, who is trying to send me off to the left and the finishing line, that I'm not part of the race.

Back onto the road and past a children's home where I spent some time on the roof about six months previously. We were trying to talk a young girl down: she was armed with a large piece of broken glass, and she was threatening to do various amounts of harm to anyone who came near her.

After explaining that I was just a fireman, and that I had left a pint of beer on the bar which was going flat, she put the glass down and came down the ladder with me.

Two miles and I'm home, one hour and 23 minutes with no walking. I soak in a hot bath feeling really pleased with myself; a large Sunday lunch and the afternoon in front of the telly with Derby County and Spurs to keep me entertained.

My legs are stiffening up now; the last thing on my mind is having to go on nights. I decide to walk to work in the hope that it will loosen up the legs.

Day 2: Rest day

I arrive home from work feeling really tired; we didn't have any shouts last night or this morning. This has been a really quiet tour. I have taken tonight off and then start 12 days' holiday.

Spend the morning tidying and hoovering. Eve and I have decided to take the dogs out to the New Forest this afternoon. We spend a really enjoyable couple of hours walking in the forest. I'm really pleased how good my legs feel after Sunday's big run.

The forest looks beautiful at this time of year; you only

need to walk for about ten minutes before you are away from everything and everybody.

I remember being more or less in this same spot in 1976 when we had all the forest fires: how we had no serious injuries I'll never know. In one particular incident one of our fire engines was down this narrow track when the wind direction changed, and blew the fire towards the men and the fire appliance. In seconds the appliance was engulfed in flames, while the firemen lay on the path as the fire jumped over them.

They were luckily all ok, but the appliance needed a respray.

Day 3: 30-minute run

Off to see Bob Donovan this morning so decide to walk to his clinic and back, then do my training run. Bob says that he is very pleased with the way things are coming along; he suggests the next time I go to his house where he runs a clinic, as opposed to the normal clinic. He wants to do a short run with me to see if he can help with my running action.

Feeling good, so decide to do a longer run, just in case I can't fit one in tomorrow. I'm definitely feeling fitter and really beginning to enjoy the running again. It's quite surprising how quickly you can get back into it.

I set off on a 7-mile circuit which takes in the Common, also a lot of road running, no walking and a time of 57 minutes.

A nice hot bath, then cook the meal. Eve is working all day today. I notice a few twinges in my back during the afternoon, I hope if I'm careful it will not come to anything.

I've got a parochial church council meeting this evening, of which I'm a member. We will be discussing the plans for the service when our new rector is installed. He is to join us in March: we have been told to expect about 300 people.

Day 4: 45-minute run/walk
The back feels a lot better this morning as I set off for my third trip into the countryside with Roger; binoculars around my neck, flask and sandwiches in bag and the sun shining. What more could a man ask for? Roger points out various tits, but frowns when I pretend to look into bedroom windows and says that the only tits that I will see today will be covered in feathers.

We walk about a mile across a boardwalk alongside the River Test to a hide where we spend an hour looking across the marshes. I had said earlier how much I would like to see a kingfisher, I have only ever had a glimpse of one in flight once before. The hide apparently is a good place to get a view of them.

You name it, we saw it: everything except a kingfisher. After a cup of tea and assorted sandwiches we walked to the two lakes and woods. Would you believe one of the lakes is called Kingfisher Lake? We could hear a woodpecker at work on one of the trees, so decided to hunt it down. We were very lucky we spotted five great spotted woodpeckers in flight, also hammering their beaks into trees.

It was a truly relaxing time, sitting on a fallen tree trunk, drinking tea and watching these beautiful birds at work. I was only brought back to reality when I saw two runners coming through the woods. It made me feel quite guilty sitting there when I perhaps should have been doing a training run.

We took a slow walk back to the car, and home for tea. An evening sitting indoors listening to Radio Solent reports on the Saints' Rumbelows Cup quarter-final against Manchester Utd at Old Trafford. We lost 3-2: oh well, there's always next year.

Day 5: 30-minute run

I drop Eve off at work and then back home to change into my running gear. I do a good warm-up and decide to run through Millbrook Estate to Redbridge Roundabout and back home along the main road, it should be about 5 miles. As I leave home I feel really good. I've been running for twenty minutes when I reach the roundabout: the roundabout is very big and includes the end of the M271.

A few years ago we had a call to a coach involved in a road traffic accident on this roundabout. It was probably one of the worst incidents that I had ever been on. I remember us arriving to find that the coach was upright. The driver had lost control as he came to the end of the motorway and entered the roundabout. The coach hit a concrete stanchion which supports a bridge.

My task was to try and gain entry into the coach from the front, to cut through the air pipe so that we could open the main door. One of the lads who was very thin managed to climb through the driver's window and cut the pipe; we could then assist the uninjured passengers off the coach. I can remember a young girl coming off the coach and running off up the road. I gave chase and managed to get hold of her: I will always remember the fear in her eyes.

She had to be told that her mother and two other passengers had died. One was decapitated.

Back home after a long, uphill stretch and 40 minutes on the watch.

Today's pension day: not that I'm that old, I collect the pension for an elderly neighbour each week; then back home to do a bit of housework and try to get Kev out of bed. He went to Manchester last night and didn't get back until the early hours of the morning.

Kev completed his apprenticeship at Christmas in painting and decorating and was told that, due to the lack of work, his company wouldn't be taking any of their apprentices on, so he's now unemployed.

Day 6: Rest day

No running today, just as well really: I made a pig of myself last night, 5 pints and a doner kebab.

Every Thursday night is drum practice; I'm a member of the Fire Brigade Pipes and Drums Corps, which was set up in 1984 for the opening of the new headquarters by Her Majesty The Queen.

We attend charity events, open days etc. and travel about quite a bit. Well, you can imagine, after a practice or an event we like a pint or two. Over the last year we have had three trips to Wales where we performed at a passing out parade, and two open days.

Day 7: 45 minutes of run/walk

Up bright and early this morning and feeling good so decide to do Sunday's run today. It suggests in the training schedule that anyone who feels stiff and tired could get on their bike and do a ride for at least an hour. If not, then design another new route and walk/run for 1.5 hours. I decide to do the run: if I'm stiff tomorrow, I'll do the ride then.

I leave home and run along a cycle track to Eling, where there's a beautiful old watermill. Along the front and through the village into Totton and through the shopping precinct on a Saturday morning.

At one stage I thought I was doing the hurdles as I jumped over shopping trolleys. After a few words of encouragement, good and bad, I'm back onto the quiet roads of Testwood; past the police station and fire station, then onto a pub called The Salmon Leap to find a small track which leads to the River Test. So far, so good, feeling good and I've been running for 45 minutes.

I'm now in the same area as I was on Wednesday when I was out with Roger birdwatching. I run across the boardwalk to Test Lane and onto the cycle track again. I arrive home after 1 hour 32 minutes on the clock and no walking. I soak in a hot bath feeling very pleased with myself. It's not quite a month since I began the training and I'm up to 10-11-mile mark.

A snack lunch, and then an afternoon of doing bits and pieces around the house with one ear on the radio, listening to Radio Solent and the Saints' fourth-round FA Cup match away to Coventry.

Eve and I are going out for a meal tonight with four good friends, which we are looking forward to. Mike and his wife June are old friends. Mike was a fireman when I joined the watch. He left after serving 12 years, and was one of the best firemen I knew.

Phil and Sheelagh we have known for about 12 years. Phil joined our watch as a new recruit; I sort of took him under my wing. He's now a sub-officer at training school, so I must have done him a bit of good.

Phil's always been a bit of a practical joker, and you never quite know what he's going to get up to next. It should be a great evening.

CHAPTER 5

TWELVE WEEKS TO GO

Day 1: 1.5 walk/run; or bike ride for 1.5 hours

Wake up this morning with a hangover and I feel pleased that I did today's run yesterday. What a great evening it turned out to be: a lot of booze, good food and a lot of reminiscing.

I think I'll opt for a bike ride after church. Back home from church, a quick cup of tea, and it's out on Kev's bike for an hour. I decide to head to Nursling and the country lanes.

It's quite a cold day and drizzling with rain. Why do they have saddles on racing bikes that are made so hard? It feels like sitting on a lump of wood.

I can see a horse and rider in front of me, and as I approach, I wonder how to get past without frightening the horse.

I try a couple of loud coughs, but they don't seem to hear me. I take a wide berth and just as I get level with the horse, it catches a glimpse of me and rears up. The young lady rider manages to control the horse. I apologise and pedal on. I come to a fork in the road and decide to take the left fork: after cycling for about a mile I come to a dead end.

I turn around and head back to the fork. As I come bounding round the corner I come face-to-face with the rider and the horse which didn't know what to do. It jumped so much I thought the rider was bound to fall off. She managed to hang on, and made some very unladylike comments.

My next big mistake was after seeing two young lads up

in front on bikes, I decide to race them. I came up behind them at full speed and as I overtook them I shouted, "The Winner!"

What a mistake, these two young lads came racing up alongside me on the inside, no matter how hard I pedalled, I just couldn't get past them. I saw some roadworks in front with traffic lights controlling them. The lights were green, so I decided a mad dash through the lights and hopefully get rid of these two lads; just before I reached the lights they changed to red.

There was no way I could stop in time, so I cut inside the cones by the roadworks just as a workman is climbing out of a large hole. He ends up jumping back into the hole shouting obscenities at me.

I glanced back over my shoulder and saw the two lads stopped at the traffic lights laughing like mad. Well, at least I had made someone's day.

Home in time for a nice roast, and then a couple of hours in front of the telly to watch the live match between Arsenal and Leeds which ended in a 0-0 draw.

Day 2: Rest day

Another cold, damp day. No running today so decide to do a walk with Eve through the Plantation and take the two dogs. They love it, in and out of the trees, in the river, and then a roll in the mud. The pair of them are covered in thick mud; as usual, I have forgotten to bring a towel or cloth to wipe them off before putting them back in the car. They both stink and leave the inside of the car covered in mud and smelling of a swamp.

We get home and I have to spend two hours cleaning

and disinfecting the car, ready to take Miss Cave, an elderly neighbour, to the hospital in the afternoon.

I drop her at the orthopaedic clinic at 1.30 and prepare myself for a long wait in the car. I have a newspaper, and my book, *It Shouldn't Happen to a Vet*, by James Herriot; but spend most of the time watching people trying to find parking spaces in this very busy hospital.

They stop anywhere and everywhere if it will save a 50-metre walk from the car park. They seem to stop no matter who or what they block.

Miss Cave comes out of hospital at 3.30, not too bad, only 2 hours. The radio in the car packed up while I was waiting; hope it's just a fuse.

Talking about radios, we used to have a leading fireman on our watch who would book mobile in an Indian accent, and then close down in a Welsh accent: it used to confuse our control room staff no end.

We have a very strict radio procedure, but during the forest fires of 1976 it was so busy one afternoon, our control room operators were telling urgent callers to wait while they spoke to urgent, urgent callers. How they coped I'll never know.

During all of this, a part-time fireman came on the radio to ask control if they would phone his wife, and ask her to pick up the sausages as he was rather busy. I think he and his family went hungry that night.

Day 3: 35-minute run/walk

Eve dropped me at Bob's clinic this morning so I could do a run straight after. Felt really good as I left the clinic. The run felt like one of the very first runs that I had done, really heavy legs, no stamina: it became a mental battle to keep going. I managed to make it home in 37 minutes. As I washed and changed, I felt my legs really stiffening up. A quick cup of tea, and then off shopping with Eve.

We decide to go to Eastleigh and have a look around the Swan Centre, a large indoor shopping mall, and then to pay a visit to my nan.

I spend five minutes knocking on the front door with no reply. I decide to try and get around the back. My nan is 91 years old and lives alone and keeps the gate locked and tied up. I manage to squeeze through a gap that I have made and try to peer through the window, but the nets are so thick I can't see through them.

I knock on the window and hear her shout, "I'm coming!" Apparently she had fallen asleep after her lunch, and because she is so deaf she couldn't hear us knocking on the door. What a relief.

We arrive home and it's off to The Dell for the Saints v Coventry replay. Saints play really well and win 2-0 with the reward of a home tie in the next round of the FA Cup to either Forest or Newcastle.

Day 4: 50-minute run/walk

Eve really has to force me out of the house this morning: my legs ache and I don't feel like doing anything. I set off thinking I really don't want to run the marathon anyway.

After a mile or so, my legs loosen up, and my breathing is settling down. I begin to enjoy the run.

I have to change my route slightly when I see a rather

unfriendly Rottweiler waiting on the other side of a gate that I need to use. I carry on past the hospital heading towards the Plantation where I turn right, and down into the sports centre. A check on the watch, 30 minutes done. I leave the sports centre by a very steep hill which really makes the legs hurt and the lungs burn.

I head towards the Common, and run through it. I have a mile left to run and have been running for 52 minutes. I arrive home after 1 hour 32 minutes.

I spend a couple of minutes stretching to try and stop the stiffness; then a hot bath, a cup of tea and then set off with Eve for a drive to Calshot where we intend to do a five-mile circular walk.

We really enjoy the walk and I manage to point out one or two different birds to Eve. It's been trying to snow all day, but not really coming to anything.

We are off to pictures tonight to see *Home Alone*: I'm dreading picking up the tickets. I phoned yesterday and booked them on Visa and purchased 6 tickets: why, I don't know, it should have been 4. Eve phoned and changed the purchase to 4. Today Julie and her friend say that they can no longer make it, so phoned and changed it once again to 2. I can imagine the people in the booking office sitting waiting to see this idiot who doesn't have a clue collect his tickets.

I arrive at the ticket office and spend 10 minutes in the wrong queue before getting the tickets.

I decide to go to the loo before the film starts; a young usher comes into the toilet with his fingers bleeding. He tells me that somebody had shut his fingers in a door. I'm holding his hand looking at the fingers when someone else comes in, he just said sorry and left again. Anyway we enjoyed the film.

Day 5: 35-minute run

I decide to do the run later today, as Eve and I want to have a look around Totton, I also want to drive around the Totton Half-Marathon course, just to refresh my memory of the route. I want to run it over the weekend.

I drive the route; it really does seem a long distance. I have run this half-marathon 4 or 5 times in the past with my best time of 1 hour 31 minutes; but normally around 1 hour 40 to 1.48.

We get home from shopping, I go and collect Miss Cave's pension. She tells me how the police had arrived at her home because a neighbour could not make her hear when they knocked on the door.

I remember when a neighbour knocked on my door to say that they couldn't make Miss Cave hear, and she hadn't been seen for a while. I climbed over a fence into her back garden, opened her back door, and just managed to stop her hitting me over the head with a saucepan.

I pop up to the fire station to sort out the catering for the next tour, and then out for a run.

It feels just like Tuesday, heavy legs and heavy breathing. I had planned a 4-mile circuit which takes me 29 minutes. So I must have picked up my pace at least. I'm not going to worry about the 6 minutes I owe. It must balance out.

Day 6: Rest day

An early start today, I've got to drive to Bournemouth to pick up John, a colleague, and have him back at the local hospital by 8.30 am. He's having a vasectomy, an operation I remember well.

For me it ended with three weeks off work, a bad infection, with bruising from my navel to the top of my legs.

I try to cheer John up on the journey by telling him what happened to me, and that it's the after-pain that's the worse. I'm only trying to get my own back from when I was in hospital for my back operation; he came to visit just after the operation, and kept asking Eve if she thought I would live because I looked so ill.

I was also with John when he had to have a finger amputated. We had a call to a fire in Totton: just as we arrived a wall collapsed on a part-time fireman. A large piece of wall fell on John's finger as we were trying to rescue the fireman, crushing it badly. After weeks of various treatments and plaster casts, they decided it needed to be amputated.

I visited John in hospital the night before the operation: he had drawn a smiling face on the nail of the finger that had to be amputated.

One of John's favourite tricks after the operation was to put on a pair of gloves with a pencil in the gap for the missing finger. He would then pretend to snap the finger in half to the horrified looks of anyone who was around.

I get a call from the hospital at lunchtime to say that I can collect John. As I arrive, he is being told by a nurse that he will need to produce a specimen in so many weeks, and gives him a small glass jar, to which he replies, "I can pee more than that." The nurse starts to explain when she realises that he's having her on.

I try to drive over as many bumps as I can on the way

home. I manage to get a few shouts of pain before I deliver him safely home.

I intend to have a nice easy evening, ready to try and run around a half-marathon course tomorrow morning. I have a bit of pain in my back this evening so will have to see how I am in the morning.

Day 7: 50-minute run/walk

Because I'm back at work tomorrow, I intend to do Sunday's 2-hour run today, and today's 50-minute run tomorrow. (I really do complicate things.)

Up early to attempt to run a half-marathon course, before helping with some repair work at the church at 10.30 am.

I set off at 7 am on one of Southampton's old marathon courses. We had a very severe frost last night, and all the puddles from yesterday's rain have frozen solid. I shorten my step, and pick my way around the ice, and into the city centre. Through the city and down towards the waterfront; I begin to wish that I had worn gloves, my hands are freezing, my back feels better this morning and my legs are feeling good.

Back towards the city centre and three miles completed; I now start a long, slightly uphill two-mile stretch towards the sports centre, past the Common.

Five miles done and I feel quite good. I intend not to look at my watch at all, but just concentrate on my running.

I now face a couple of miles of steep uphill and downhill stretches. My hands feel warmer now and I'm really sweating. Seven miles completed, and I now head out into the country and a fairly flat four miles. A car horn beeps, and I recognise a fireman on another watch heading towards work. I'm tempted to check the watch, but manage to leave it in my pocket.

A long, uphill stretch which leads me to the fire station and the 11.5-mile mark. I'm feeling really tired now, legs aching. As I pass the station I quicken my pace and try to look fit and relaxed, and prepared to wave to the men on duty: they didn't see me.

Twelve miles done, and absolutely shattered. I keep thinking about having a walk, but manage to plod on to home and have a hot bath.

I lie in the bath feeling quite miserable, 2 hours 20 seconds, and absolutely shattered. Will I ever be ready to run twice that distance?

Off to the church where a group of us intend to take down a large illuminated cross, which is 80 feet in the air, to replace the fluorescent tubes and repaint. The work involves three men in the bell tower lowering, and two men at ground level pulling on guide ropes to keep the cross from the wall. It sounds simple, but takes about two hours to get down. It will be repaired at leisure and put back up in a few weeks.

I have to come home and have another bath. I was ankle-deep in pigeon droppings in the bell tower.

On the way home I decide to stop at a disabled neighbour's house to put a new washing line up.

The daughter goes down the garden to open the gate for me, but falls over the dog and can't get up. I have to split my ladder so that I can go up one side of the fence and down the other.

Now the fun, or should I say the strain, starts, for the daughter weighs 18 stone. A lot of pulling and sweating and she's on her feet, with no serious damage to body or garden.

Home for lunch and an easy afternoon listening to the football. I wish I hadn't bothered: Saints are losing 4-0 at half-time away to Sheffield Utd.

I'm off to Hayling Island this evening with the Fire Service Drum Corps to play at a 40th birthday party.

Saints lost 4-1.

CHAPTER 6

ELEVEN WEEKS TO GO

Day 1: 2-hour walk/run

As I said yesterday, I changed Saturday and Sunday's training schedule around so that I should be doing a 50-minute run/walk today.

Back to work today and I'm feeling really stiff, so decide to have a rest day.

0.859 Duty watch Parade, I'm detailed to drive the Hydraulic Platform and also duty cook. I spend the morning cooking a roast lunch for nine, which turns out well. We have an early lunch today because we are going on a visit this afternoon to a new catamaran that is in the dry dock.

I drive the HP down through Shirley and into the docks. Apparently nobody knew we were coming so there's a delay while they find someone to show us around.

The ship has just won the Blue Riband for the fastest crossing of the Atlantic. A quick guided tour and then it's back to the station to clean three fire engines, sweep the floor, cup of tea, and it's time to hand over to the night watch.

I walk home and it's beginning to freeze already. The legs are feeling better now, but I don't think an extra rest day will hurt.

Day 2: Rest day

Another day at work. It's hard having to do two days. Driving the water Tender today. After a quick cup of tea, it's full kit for drill. Because of the freezing conditions the sub-officer decided that we would drill inside today.

The task is to rescue a casualty stuck at the top of the fireman's pole, but we are not allowed to touch the floor.

By constructing a bridge out of ladders, we make our way across the three appliances that are parked to reach the casualty and bring him back the same way.

A very interesting and beneficial drill.

11 am and it's tea break followed by physical training. I manage to get 55 minutes of running and walking in, which makes me feel better after missing yesterday's training.

Time for lunch, then an afternoon of testing and painting hydrants.

I remember one day when we were out painting hydrants, one of the chaps was told to cut part of a hedge away because it was blocking the indicator plate. Well, he got a bit carried away and made this large hole in the person's hedge, who later complained to the Fire Brigade. When he was interviewed by a senior officer, he just apologised and said, "I just got carried away." The officer then had to go and apologise to the rather distraught owner of the hedge.

Day 3: 20 minutes of running. But make it sharper than any previous run (well, that's what the book says.)

The problem was I just didn't get 20 minutes spare to run, let alone a faster one.

I went up to London last night with a mate of mine who drives a lorry load of fish to various places, ending up at Billingsgate. He asked if I would like to go with him for the ride, which I did. I found myself going over a large part of the London Marathon course. I didn't arrive home until 3 am.

A good lie-in, then off to see Bob Donovan, collect Eve from work, and then do the shopping. Something to eat, and then off to work.

I'm off to the AGM of the Fire Brigade Benevolent Fund this evening. Although I thought I was going to miss my lift when we picked up a chimney fire at 18.30. Luckily it was straightforward and I got to the meeting on time.

Back to the station, and egg and chips for supper. Two calls during the night, and off home at 09.00.

Day 4: An extra rest day

I decide to do yesterday's 20 minutes today: it gives me a chance to try out my new running shoes, I have been needing some for quite some time, but kept putting it off until Eve took control.

I set off feeling tired because of nights, but I make a conscious effort to run faster than normal. All goes well for the first ten minutes; I then feel a slight pull in my left calf muscle, nothing serious, just a nagging ache. I finish the run and my lungs are really puffing. I notice my leg is beginning to hurt a bit more, but just hope it won't come to much.

A bit of housework, pick Eve up from work, and an afternoon of dozing in front of the TV watching a video that Eve recorded for me last night.

Day 5: 45-minute continuous run

I spend the morning doing a bit of housework and preparing the evening meal. Eve is working all day today, so I try and get things done in the morning so that I can train this afternoon.

I drop Julie at college at 14.00 and then drive to the

Common. We had a bit of snow last night and everywhere is frozen. I decide to run through the Common and up to the sports centre; it's started snowing again and getting quite slippery underfoot. A long, uphill stretch past the golf club, not a golfer in sight.

It was about here the last time I was training for the London Marathon that I tore an ankle ligament. It's about three miles from home, and a long hobble when there is nobody at home to phone to come and get you.

No pulls or strains today, even my left calf is feeling good.

The snow is really getting heavy now as I approach a really steep, uphill stretch which goes on for 300 metres or so. I make it to the top and up and across a road bridge: the steps are really treacherous, and the snow is so thick now I can hardly see where I am going.

I feel warm apart from my head, where I realise the snow has frozen on the little bit of hair that I have.

Back into the Common with about a mile to go, I decide to come off the path and onto the grass where I hope to get a better grip. A big mistake: the ruts and frozen mud are making it very uneven.

Back to the car at last: once inside I look in the rear-view mirror and notice that my eyebrows are frozen. I have to get out of the car again to scrape the snow and ice off the windscreen and rear window.

A slow, slippery drive home, then a long soak in a hot bath to defrost. I decide to give drum practice a miss tonight and have a night in front of the fire. I'm supposed to be birdwatching tomorrow, but if this weather continues I will have to give it a miss.

Day 6: Rest day

Woke up today to thick snow everywhere, not the sort of weather for birdwatching, so phoned Roger to let him know.

Spent the morning doing housework, quite successful really, washed all the floors, hoovered and made all the beds, and even managed to mend a kitchen drawer.

Went to pick Eve up from work. As I was waiting in the car park I saw a beautiful-looking bird, the feathered sort. I looked it up when I got back home to discover that it was a redwing, which is quite common.

A quick snack, then it's off shopping. The main roads are clear, but the side roads are treacherous. I call into the fire station to drop off the catering, then home for tea.

We drive to Eastleigh in the evening to my brother and sister-in-law and spend a couple of hours playing with David and Andrew, our nephews.

More snow is forecast for tonight. I'm hoping to do a half-marathon course tomorrow, but will wait until the morning to see what the snow is like, and then an hour run on Sunday.

We are going up to my parents' house for tea tomorrow along with my brother and his family. My brother Garry is very laid back, nothing seems to make him panic. A couple of months ago he was in his back garden cleaning his football boots, when his wife Dulcie came running out to say that the oven was on fire. Garry in his calm, collective way said, "Give Terry a ring and ask him what to do."

Dulcie phoned 999, rescued their son Paul and the budgie, and awaited Eastleigh fire crew to put out the Yorkshire pudding while Garry finished off his boots.

FIREMAN ON THE RUN

Day 7: 1-hour run/walk

No snow overnight, but still frozen snow everywhere. I intend to run a half-marathon route today, then do the 1-hour run on Sunday.

A good warm-up, but couldn't find my stopwatch, so borrowed Kev's. I decided to run the same route as last week, but the opposite way. I set the watch and head off, treading warily on the frozen pavement towards the fire station, a bit of abuse as I pass the station as I give the lads a victory salute.

The pavement is very slippery here and contemplate running on the road, then decide against it as the traffic is very heavy.

Head out into the country now and have to run on the roads due to the lack of pavements, it's quite slushy here and I start to slip and slide a bit. I wonder if it was a good idea to do the run today; but they say that the weather is going to last at least a week, and I don't think I can afford to miss a week's training at this stage.

I plod on to the main road where I have to run on the grass verge: the snow is 2 to 3 inches deep; although very soft, it makes the going heavy. A steep bank to get down, which I manage without any mishap, and then back to compacted snow and ice on the pavements.

About 5 miles done, and like last week I intend not to look at the watch until I get home. A brief spell on the Common with virgin snow, then out onto the Avenue for a 2-mile stretch into the city centre.

I approach the city centre with about 9 to 10 miles done, all the pavements have been gritted, and thanks to a lot of hard work by the council staff, are free of snow and ice.

I'm feeling tired now, but because I'm running through the city centre with all the shoppers about, I pick up my pace and head towards the waterfront.

Along the waterfront, and around the backstreets of Southampton to Shirley, 12 miles done. It's funny how the lack of people here makes my pace slow considerably. I must be really vain, or perhaps just knackered.

Home at last, and no walking or falling over: what an achievement in these conditions. I look at the watch and it says 7 hours and 20 minutes; I know I was slow, but think the watch is on the blink.

A long, hot soak in the bath, then an afternoon of not doing much. We have to pick Julie up at 5.30 from her Saturday job, then drive to Eastleigh for a meal at my parents.

CHAPTER 7

TEN WEEKS TO GO

Day 1: 2-hour run/walk

I did this yesterday, so today I should be doing the 1-hour run/walk. Last night was even colder, down to minus 13, and as you can imagine, the roads and pavements are like skating rinks.

Off to church this morning, and it's beginning to snow again. We decide to take the car and drive very carefully, but still manage to skid sideways on the road. The congregation is very small today, and the church is very cold. I don't suppose it helps that we are in the middle of having a new roof put on.

I'm asked today if I would give a talk on the work of the Fire Brigade to the Women's Fellowship in May. I will have to get permission from a senior officer.

I remember a few years ago, a recruit on his first evening was found giving a talk to a local youth club on the Fire Brigade. He's no longer with us.

Home from church and it's far too dangerous to run at the moment, so decide to take my running gear with me when we visit my sister-in-law this afternoon for tea, with the hope that things will improve, and I may be able to get out then.

A bit better this afternoon, so set off to run around the Eastleigh 10k route. It's about half a mile away, so I will do a total of about 7 miles. The first mile is ok, clear pavements, but after that it's a bit countryish, and the snow is very compact and slippery, also uphill. I try running on the road, which is clear, but the volume of traffic forces me back onto the pavement. My legs are aching a bit from yesterday, but nothing too bad.

It worked out just right; I arrived back on the hour and felt pretty good. A nice tea and a pleasant chat, then it's time to drive home and an early night.

Day 2: Rest day

Back to work and decide to walk in these conditions.

08.59 Duty Watch parade. I'm detailed to drive the Hydraulic platform, a good check of the lockers to make sure nothing is missing, check the diesel, oil and water, then sign to say that the vehicle is ok. I always walk around it to check for dents or scratches before doing this.

A quick cup of tea, then it's full kit for drill which today consists of dressing in BA and chemical protection suits. This takes us up to 11 o'clock and tea break.

After tea I ask if I can take the HP into the yard for familiarisation. I attempt to put down the jacks which stabilise the vehicle, and one of the four will not move. We inform Workshops and the machine is taken off the run until they can get here to repair it.

In the meantime the bells go down and the two pumps disappear on a fire call, leaving me alone on the station. I'm told by the staff office that if Workshops can't repair the HP I will have to go to Southsea to pick up a spare.

St. Mary's water tender arrives to stand by at our station, while our two machines are dealing with a fire in a Portakabin containing acetylene cylinders. Trust me to miss it.

One crew arrives back just on lunchtime, the other about 20 minutes later.

After lunch there's still no sign of Workshops, so a staff sub-officer drives me down to Southsea to collect the brigade spare HP.

The last time I was at Southsea fire station was about five or six years ago when I took part in a Fire Brigade 5-mile road race.

I collect the HP, and after checking the inventory I drive back to Southampton where we have to transfer pieces of equipment from our HP to the spare. After about ten minutes we phone control and book it "On the Run".

Time for a quick wash and brush-up, and then a twenty-minute walk home. I was pleased to see Eve and the two dogs waiting for me outside the station: she thought that all three of them could do with a walk.

Eve has been told today that her application to work full-time has been agreed, and she will start on March 1st.

Day 3: 20-25 minutes of sharp running

Another walk to work this morning, I'm riding BA on the Water Tender Ladder; this means that if we get a fire I will be the first in. It makes a pleasant change from driving all the time.

We spend the morning having a lecture from a station officer on carrying out petroleum visits, in other words what to look out for when we do an inspection on a petrol station.

The station officer who is taking the lecture joined the same time as me. I remember senior officers saying he would never make a fireman because he was too puny-looking and had no strength. He ended up top recruit, and like I said he is now a station officer.

The water tender had two calls this morning, one to flooding; we are going to get a lot of these as the thaw sets in, and one to an automatic fire alarm.

I've been given permission to talk to the Women's Fellowship in May and booked the video and TV.

The portable TV has a 26-inch screen which takes six men to lift.

I spend five minutes during the morning watching the recruits in the drill yard. They only started yesterday; today is known as Hose Tuesday where they spend the morning learning how to run out hose. The instructors seem to get great pleasure in seeing how many they can get to collapse through exhaustion.

Just after lunch we get a call to the local maternity hospital where a sprinkler in an underground car park has activated. It turns out to be nothing.

I'm hoping to do my training this evening, but have promised to go shopping with Eve first.

We just started a game of volleyball when we get a call to one of the high-rise blocks of the nurses' home at the local hospital. We get to the room involved, and find a distraught nurse sitting on her bed saying, "I only phoned the hospital switchboard to report an overheated plug."

There were three fire engines, a hydraulic platform and emergency tender, two police cars and an ambulance.

Eve picked me up from work; she had done all the shopping during the afternoon. I love that woman.

A quick cup of tea, then I change into my running gear. I

really don't feel like training at this time of day. I'm going to do tomorrow's training today; it says your first proper fartlek training; no more than 30 minutes, once or twice your lungs should be heaving. Once or twice, they must be joking, my lungs were heaving from the first fast run, right until I got back home some 22 minutes later. I started with a gentle jog of 8-10 minutes, then did a very fast run, then a gentle jog, then a fast run and so on for about 8-10 minutes. It was the hardest training session I have done. Twenty-two minutes of this was enough for me; a soak in a hot bath was the icing on the cake.

Day 4: 30 minutes of fartlek
I did this session yesterday, today I'm going to see Bob Donovan who is coming running with me, and hopefully will put right what I'm doing wrong.

My brother Garry phoned last night to say that my nan has had a burst pipe in the roof space, so I must call in and see her this morning.

I drive to Bob's home in Twyford, and we spend the first five minutes stretching, and then out into the unknown. Bob lives in a very nice area, and within 500 yards we are into a country lane. We start off at a slow pace with him running behind me. We then take the pace up slowly, he then comes alongside me and shows me how to relax my arms: by doing this it relaxes my legs.

We keep running for about 20 minutes with him putting various bad habits right. It's then back indoors and various stretching and relaxing exercises. I leave feeling really good.

As I pull up outside my nan's house, she opens the front

door before I'm out of the car; she tells me that she has been looking out of the window for the nurse who is coming to give her 2-monthly injection. As I walk into her lounge, or sitting room as she likes to call it, I notice the damp patches on her ceiling. She said that a pipe had burst, flooding her bedroom, and then through the ceiling into her sitting room.

Her neighbour had taken all her bedding and dried it in their tumble dryer. I checked the bedroom which was now dry. Her sitting room was fine apart from the damp patch on the ceiling. She had plenty of food, and had refused to move out and spend a couple of days with my parents.

Bombing couldn't get her out in the last war, so a little bit of water certainly won't budge her now.

I arrive home just before Eve; we have a quick cup of tea and a snack, and then drive to the Plantation to give the two dogs a good walk. It's then home and get ready for work.

Off to work, and another duty on the HP. I look out of the window during the evening and watch the recruits scrubbing the yard. I know that they need to learn discipline, but this is ridiculous.

Day 5: 50 minutes of running

A quiet night, but I still feel shattered. I help cook the breakfast, while the others clean the fire engines and mop the floor ready for changeover at 9 o'clock.

I brought my running gear to work last night, so I change into this and do a good warm-up before setting off on a 6-mile route. The first couple of miles are really hard-going; I try to put into practice some of the things that Bob told me yesterday: they seem to help in getting me going. Training after nights seems to be a bad time, but I have got to do it.

Bob explained to me yesterday that if I can learn to relax my arms, then my legs will relax; my elbows relate to my knees, and my wrists to my ankles. I manage to complete the run in exactly one hour, which includes stopping at a veg shop and buying a swede.

Home to a hot bath, make a casserole for tea, a quick hoover around, and then off to pick Eve up from work so that we can drive to Eastleigh and have a look around the market.

I take a Valentine's card and a plastic red rose, which I give to Eve as she gets in the car, just as someone walks past with a dozen red roses. Well, it's the thought that counts.

Home from Eastleigh and I pop into Miss Cave to give her her pension, and to put a new battery into one of her smoke detectors. An hour later, I come out unable to stop the detector from sounding all the time. I take it down in the end so I can take it to work with the hope that someone may know what is causing it.

A plate of casserole and then off to work. We have got the deputy chief fire officer coming tonight to take us for drill: you would think he'd have something better to do on a freezing winter's night.

Another duty on the HP. We all line up for the deputy chief who is accompanied by a divisional officer who is responsible for training, and our own divisional commander.

The drill crews are one machine from each city station, plus the Emergency Tender. For the drill I'm on the Water Tender Ladder but must remain available in case the HP gets a call.

The DCFO thanks us for coming, as if we had a choice,

and explains the outline of the drill; we have to pretend that the tower is a 4-storey block of flats built over the top of a hardware shop which is well alight.

Two hours later, with everybody soaking wet, including the training officer (somebody deserves a pint for getting him wet), the drill is finished and it's off to supper.

Day 6: Rest day

I arrive home from work just after 9 am to find a note from Eve to say that the water tank is leaking. I phone the landlady, and she asks me to see our next-door neighbour who does all her plumbing work. He's out, but Christine, his wife, says he'll be home during the afternoon.

I'm off birdwatching with Roger today; we spend a very pleasant day on the Lower Test Nature Reserve.

I arrive home about 4 o'clock. Brian is in the middle of putting in a new water tank when I smell gas. I trace it to the cooker where we have a leak.

The gas emergency fitter arrives in about 15 minutes, and now we have no water or gas. I have to leave in an hour to go to headquarters where I'm playing in a display of pipes and drums.

I borrow Kev's electric razor, use the last bit of water that's in the kettle for a wash, and leave home feeling tired and hungry.

The display goes really well and we celebrate with 4 or 5 pints, and I get dropped off at home about 11 pm. Not really the preparation for tomorrow's training run.

Day 7: 50 minutes of fartlek training

I decide to try and do Sunday's training today, which is a 2-3-hour run/walk, because I won't get a spare three hours tomorrow.

I've planned a route of 16-17 miles; I set off in the car to drive to the starting point down by the River Test.

The first mile and a half is across the marshes, running along a two-planked boardwalk. This should have been simple enough, but I forgot to allow for the tide. Most of the boardwalk is a foot under water; I decide to carry on and spend 10 minutes walking through the water. In one place the water came up to my knees. I reach the other side and take off my shoes to empty the water; not an ideal start.

I'm now at the start of the Totton Half-Marathon route and set off at a steady pace around the Calmore Estate, then out into the country for the majority of this very picturesque route.

My legs are very heavy, and I wish I hadn't drunk quite so much last night. I have an awful thought that if I should pull a muscle or any injury I'm in the middle of nowhere, and the car is not at home for Eve or Kev to come and get me.

Back into civilisation with no injuries, just very tired legs. I start thinking about the boardwalk and wonder if the tide has come up any more. I decide I will swim across the boardwalk rather than run the extra 4 miles around the road if needed. Luckily the tide has dropped and I manage to run along the planks and back to the car with 2 hours 33 minutes on the watch.

When I arrive home I have a job getting out of the car, I have really stiffened up. I have also developed a bit of a cough. I do hope I'm not sickening for something.

I spend the evening sitting in front of the telly and feeling heavy and aching.

CHAPTER 8

NINE WEEKS TO GO

Day 1: 3 hours walk/run

I wake up this morning feeling heavy and a bit chesty. I'm glad I did today's big run yesterday. It should be 50 minutes of fartlek today, but I think I'll have a rest day today and see how I feel tomorrow.

Off to church with Eve this morning and I read a lesson.

Home and a mad rush to cook the Sunday dinner and tidy up. We are going to the mother-in-law's after dinner to celebrate her birthday.

We arrive an hour after everybody else: I thought they said 3 o'clock but apparently it was 2 o'clock.

Anyway, everybody was settled and watching Liverpool v Everton, which was the game on the telly. Once that was finished we had tea which was nice, everybody had bought or made something, and it was all on the table and looked quite impressive.

We arrive home about 7.30 and I feel real fluey and a bit chesty. An early night and hoping to feel better tomorrow.

Day 2: Rest day

I woke up this morning feeling a bit better and left to drive to see Bob Donovan for my session of Alexander Technique. Another good session, I leave feeling really good. I drive to the supermarket to do the catering for work. They really seem tight with carrier bags: the checkout girl gives me two carrier bags and I have to keep asking for more. I ask her if they stop the cost of carrier bags out of her wages. I didn't quite catch her reply.

I go into the station to drop off the catering, I get a few funny looks as I walk across the drill yard where the recruits are training, to put the freezer food away.

I still can't see why they need to treat human beings the way they do.

I arrive home about midday and David, a friend and colleague, calls round to see if I fancy a pint. I did, of course, and we spend a couple of hours in the local putting the world to rights.

Home for a coffee and a toasted sandwich. Dave leaves saying cheerio until tomorrow.

Eve reminds me that I need to phone the Union Jack Club in London to book a room for the Saturday night before the marathon. They are fully booked, and have been for some considerable time, the receptionist tells me, adding it's due to the London Marathon.

We are off this evening to Eve's works bowling competition. I bowl in my normal way which is pretty poor, but enjoy the evening, even if the main conversation is about insurance, which I know nothing about.

Day 3: A sharp 25 minutes

Back to work today and driving the Ladder, we spend the whole morning drilling: it was hard work but enjoyable, and the time really flies.

Two of the new lads on the watch go through their leading fireman drills. This means that they have to stand out in front and detail a drill, and then tell us what mistakes that we made.

I honestly feel that these drills should only be for firemen outside their probationary period. It seems really strange that a recruit can take a leading fireman's exam when he's not even a fireman until after his two-year probation.

In some instances you can get a man made up to leading fireman who has only been in the job for two years.

Off to lunch and the Water Tender gets a call to a car on fire towards the end of the lunch hour.

I spend an hour in the gym after lunch; I'm responsible for testing, cleaning and maintaining the multi-gym equipment, in my role as Watch Physical Training Instructor. I think that I ought to start doing more general fitness ready for the big day, at least to try and lose some weight.

At 16.00 we go off to the park for a game of football; I decide to spend the time on the running track which is adjacent to the football pitch. I decide to do 25 minutes of fartlek training, starting off by a couple of slow laps. I then up the speed for one lap, then really push it out on the straights, and jog and walk around the bends.

It's probably one of the hardest sessions that I have done, and when I finish I'm really puffing, and my legs are aching.

Back to the station where we wash all three wagons, sweep the floor and generally tidy up ready for the end of the shift.

Kev drives to pick me up, then home to a hot bath. I'm sure I'm sickening for something. I spend the evening sweating and then freezing: this has been going on for a couple of days.

Day 4: 30 minutes' fartlek

Off to work this morning and still feeling a bit shivery, I'm asked if I would like to make a Benevolent visit this morning to a fireman who has been off sick for a while. I spend a pleasant hour chatting to him and his wife, and leave a basket of fruit supplied by the Benevolent Fund.

I've been on the receiving end of this visit in the past, and I know how much it means to people to stay in touch, and know that they are not forgotten when on long-term sick. I have also visited firemen from other brigades who are in one of our local hospitals, including a chap who was here from Guernsey with a severely broken ankle.

We managed to make sure that his wife was collected from the airport and returned when needed. It's these little things that make it all worthwhile.

I used to get many visits when I was in Carmarthen General Hospital with a collapsed lung. To be miles away from loved ones, and on your own, it's surprising how a 10-minute visit from someone you have never met before can pick you up. Also the knowledge that your family are being taken care of.

They say that you can go anywhere in the world as a serving or retired fireman, and know that there is help and support if needed.

Back to work, and detailed as second man on the HP. After a quick cup of tea, John, the driver, and I drive to the local hospital to use some derelict buildings for drill.

Our first problem is the radio, which keeps us in contact with our control. It's not working properly and we are told to return to station; from then on it got progressively worse and we lost complete communications.

Luckily we were only half a mile away from the station, so we were soon back and put a new radio pack on: this corrected the fault.

We have one crew at Fawley fire station doing their quarterly breathing apparatus training, which is something we all have to do.

Just after lunch our Water Tender Ladder got sent to a chimney fire and were there until 15.00, getting their lunch at 15.30.

John and I trained on the HP in the drill yard, giving each other different targets to reach with the HP.

Physical training time, and off to the park. A good warm-up and I go to the running track while the others play football for 25 minutes. Running around a track is not my cup of tea. I find it much harder than running on the roads, I really have to force myself to keep going. I run at quite a good pace and try to remember the things Bob told me.

Back to the station and a cup of tea; as we sit around the mess table someone reminds me of the time I was at the petrol station filling up with petrol, the owners were changing the prices at the pumps as I was filling up. When I went to the kiosk to pay, I said, "You needn't think I'm going to pay your new prices, the petrol was in my tank before you changed the price." "Fair enough," said the chap. As I was leaving I said, "As a matter of interest, how much were you putting the price up to?" He replied, "I wasn't. They were going down!"

Day 5: 50 minutes' contained run

On nights today and I wake up with a bit of gyp in my back, so decide not to train. When I get these warning signs I know that if I don't take note, then I'm asking for trouble.

A physiotherapist told me after the operation that I should never exercise through pain in my back. I feel a bit dejected, what with the symptoms of a cold or flu hanging around for a few days, and now the back pain, my training is suffering and so are the family with my moods.

I manage to buy 3 lbs of onion sets today ready for the allotment, check the car for oil, water and tyre pressures, make a curry for tea, and just take things easy ready for nights.

We spend the evening doing standard tests. All pieces of equipment have to be checked and tested periodically.

Our Control phones to say that there is a large barn fire, and that our water tender will be required as a 1 am relief crew. We arrive at the barn at 00.50 and set up our lighting gear; we then run out a couple of lines of hose.

The Salvation Army are in attendance: they really do a good job feeding and watering. What we need to remember is that these people turn out with about 15 minutes' notice in all weather conditions, without payment, to supply us with refreshments.

I believe that the Fire Brigade pay for the cost of the food, but the work is voluntary. What a night, plenty of smoke, watery eyes, a chesty cough: great, this is what I joined for.

Back to the station about 4.30 am and it takes an hour to clean the mud and dirt off all the equipment and fire engine.

Day 6: Rest day

I leave work at 09.00 and call around to tell Roger that I will not be going birdwatching. Then home to bed by 09.30. I catnap and toss and turn until 14.00; then hoover just before Eve gets in at 14.30. I watch a bit of TV and dose in the chair; then it's back to work. Driving the HP tonight and a quiet time for me, although there are three calls during the shift.

Day 7: one-hour walk/run

I leave work at 09.00 and looking forward to six days off, a pleasant walk home, a couple of hours in bed, and then up for lunch.

Eve suggests that we go for a bike ride during the afternoon; so I decide if I do tomorrow's training today, which says, look up the training guide and repeat what you did a month ago.

It then says: if you don't find this easier, then send us a postcard.

Well, a month ago, I did an hour's bike ride, so today sounds good. Luckily both of our children have a decent racing bike, so we borrow these and set off for the Common.

A beautiful afternoon, although quite high winds, sees the Common full of people out enjoying themselves in these beautiful surroundings. I think of all the lads out in the Gulf, with a deadline closely approaching for a withdrawal from Kuwait. How lucky we are to be here, and how thankful we should be to the allies in the Gulf. My prayers are with them as a ground war looms.

I hope if I get called in to help with casualty handling I can cope with the horrific injuries I will obviously have to deal with.

We cycle around for an hour and a half, and back indoors to hear that the Saints are losing 1-0 away to QPR.

CHAPTER 9

EIGHT WEEKS TO GO

Day 1: Same as Day 1 of the previous month

I did this yesterday and therefore I'm doing Saturday's one-hour run/walk today.

Eve wakes me up with breakfast in bed, also with the news that the land war has started. Off to church, and as you can imagine a lot of prayers are said for the forces in the Gulf. After the service we collect some flowers that were put in the church yesterday for a wedding, and deliver them to the bride's mother, who is an old friend of Eve's. Her son-in-law is off to Germany today with the Army.

I volunteered to help during the week to paint the cross, it has been taken down to replace the fluorescent tubes and an overhaul.

I drive to Bitterne to pick Julie up. I then change into my running gear and set off towards the Common. The minute I leave home I know that this is going to be a bad run. My calf muscle in my right leg has started hurting and progressively gets worse. I realise that enough is enough and head for home, arriving 30 minutes after leaving.

I place a 2-lb packet of frozen peas on my leg, and then have Sunday lunch.

When I was having physio after my back operation, I remember a physio telling me about an elderly lady: she was told to place a frozen packet of peas on her swollen ankle. About three weeks later she arrived in the physiotherapy department with a carrier bag full of packets of frozen peas.

She explained that she didn't like peas so brought them in for somebody who did. She hadn't thought of using something other than peas.

I spend the evening with my leg raised, feeling sorry for myself.

Day 2: Rest day

Just as well: my leg still hurts, and there is no way I can run today. Kevin leaves for Wigan this morning; I pick Eve up from work at lunchtime to be told that, due to the economic situation, they won't be able to take her on full-time. This is very annoying, because she was told two weeks ago that she had the job.

We take Bouncer, one of our two dogs, to the vet this afternoon for his booster injection.

I'm off to The Dell this evening for the FA Cup game with Nottingham Forest. Saints draw 1-1 and now face a replay at Forest next Monday.

Kev phoned to say that he got redirected to Coventry, and will be there until next Monday, working a 15-hour night. Poor Kev.

Day 3: 50-Minute medium run

I got up this morning with my leg feeling a bit better, but not quite right. Eve is home all day today; I set off to see Bob at the clinic.

I have never known Bob to be miserable, and today he's his usual happy self. We start off by going through a few lunges and other exercises. We spend a fair bit of time putting the world to rights, and I tell him about my leg. He said that

I did the right thing in stopping. He said that in general if the pain gets worse it's time to stop.

He spends a fair bit of time working on my legs, which in his opinion are not as flexible or stress-free as my upper body, and therefore more likely to have aches or pains while the change takes place.

I decide to do a gentle run and see how the leg holds out and how far I can get. I have my 10p in my pocket to phone Eve if needed.

A gentle mile to the Common, and so far, so good. Through the Common and into the sports centre for a short distance, then back onto the road with 25 minutes done and just a dull ache. Down through a wood, across a boardwalk, then through a playing field, back onto the road, uphill to the fire station with 40 minutes done. This is an improvement: it used to take me 45 minutes to run this. I carry on past the fire station and head towards my allotment: as I look across I glimpse Bill digging away. Apparently he's even there on Christmas Day.

Another two miles, and home on the hour, with my leg just feeling a dull ache.

A quick bath, then it's off to Sainsbury's with Eve to do the catering as well as our own shopping. We drop the catering at the fire station, pop into Shirley to pick up a few bits and pieces, and then home.

Julie is having her hair permed in the kitchen, so I'm forced to sit in the lounge and read the papers. What a hard life.

Roger phones to check that everything is ok for tomorrow. We arrange to meet between 9 and 9.30 to go birdwatching.

Day 4: Take an extra rest day

What more could a man want? An extra rest day. I meet Roger about 9 o'clock and we set off to Romsey to call into the office of the Hampshire and Isle of Wight Naturalist Trust to collect maps and leaflets of their local sights.

We decide to go to Ampfield and arrive after about 15 minutes in the pouring rain. We spend an hour or so walking through a small part of the site and decide we are getting too wet to enjoy it, so we leave and drive to the hide on the Lower Test.

We spend an hour sitting in the hide drinking tea and eating sandwiches, as well as drying out. The rain stops and we leave the hide for a walk to the woods and lakes. It is really a quiet day as far as birds are concerned; nevertheless, it's still one of the most relaxing days, with a walk of five to six miles spread over a period of about six hours.

I arrive home in time for tea, and Eve is making the most of Kev being away by blitzing his bedroom. Eve asks me to carry a set of weights from his bedroom into ours.

I decide to start using weights again to try and improve my general fitness; I haven't really touched any weights since my lung collapsed.

I remember when I was in hospital in Wales. I was in a chest ward with people coughing up phlegm all day and night. There was one old chap next to me who had chronic bronchitis and emphysema, as well as asthma.

He was a lovely old chap who used to sleep all day and sit up all night either talking to me, or sitting on the commode or eating crisps, sometimes doing both together.

I used to wake up with Reg sitting on the commode

with his packet of crisps, lying on my bed while he tucked into them.

The nurses would come and push him back to the side of his bed, but as soon as they went he would wheel himself back to me, a toilet roll in one hand and a sandwich in the other. He got quite emotional when I was discharged.

An evening in front of the telly and trying to help Julie with her A level project.

Day 5: one-hour slow run

A quick hoover of the lounge and hallway, a good warm-up and then off for the 1-hour run. I feel quite good this morning: a dull ache in my right calf, but nothing to worry about.

I spend the first 35 minutes running along various roads I haven't been along before; but I know they will lead me out to the Common. Into the Common, and all the way around. I'm confronted by a dog but manage to stare him out and carry on running with a regular glance over my shoulder.

Into the cemetery where I once told a new recruit that this was actually the dead centre of Southampton: he had written this in the diary that he had to keep, before realising the joke.

Home in one hour and one minute, and then soak in a hot bath.

After a sandwich I pop down to the church to clean and rub down the cross ready for painting. There is a funeral service later so I only stay for half an hour.

I decide to drive down to my allotment for the first time this year. It has been completely dug ready for planting, but due to the wet conditions I'm holding back a bit before putting my onion sets in. I spend an hour chatting to a couple of chaps down there, and then drive back home.

The rest of the afternoon is spent cleaning the car inside and out. It certainly needed it.

A fireman from another station asked if I could have a chat with his wife who has just had the same back operation as me: she is feeling a bit low. I'm going to drive over to see her tonight, and hopefully tell her what to expect over the next few months.

The poor woman: she had been told that her job was finished, the same as they told me, and that she really would have to change her lifestyle.

I know the surgeons deal with this sort of thing all the time, but I do feel that they have lost a lot of the human side of things. Or do they say these things to deliberately set a challenge to prove them wrong?

Anyway, I hope that Eve and I had given her the determination to prove them wrong.

Day 6: Rest day

I spend most of the morning making phone calls and filling in forms for Kev, to enable him to stop claiming some things and start claiming others. I have got all the forms ready for him to sign when he gets home, which is either Sunday or Monday. He will only be home for one evening, and then he is away again.

I pick Eve up from work and spend some time during the afternoon planning a big walk/run session for tomorrow. Hopefully I will have a good night at work tonight. I intend to do three hours straight from work, ending up at Lyndhurst where Eve is going to drive with the two dogs and pick me up.

A quiet night for me on the HP, although the other lads had three calls.

A message has come from the chief officer stating that they may be asked to send men out to Kuwait to help with the refinery fires.

Day 7: 45 minutes in the park and enjoy running

Well, I'm going to do this tomorrow after my second night. Today I'm going to do Sunday's 3-hour run/walk.

I leave the station at 9.15 am after a good warm-up and set off at a steady pace through the Millbrook housing estate, heading towards the main road and along the cycle track and walkway to Eling. Over the Eling toll bridge and off out into the countryside. I have 50p in change, a mate from work has given me his telephone number, and a Mars bar in my running top pocket.

Brian, whom I work with, said he will be home all day, so if I get any problems, give him a ring and he'd pick me up if I couldn't get hold of Eve, who is doing the shopping before driving to Lyndhurst to meet me at 12.30.

The sun is starting to shine, so I take my waterproof top off, and after a great deal of hard work, try to fold it up while still running; it's one of those that folds up inside one of the pockets, and then there is a strap to put it around your waist. I eventually succeed without having to stop running.

Through Marchwood village, and then across the main road, which has been the scene of many a road traffic accident, and into the beautiful New Forest, heading towards the Beaulieu Road.

FIREMAN ON THE RUN

I pass the Beaulieu Road Hotel with a signpost saying 4 miles to Lyndhurst. I arrive at Lyndhurst with 2 hours 10 minutes on the watch. I walk for ten minutes and eat the much-travelled Mars bar. I then spend the next 20 minutes walking and running through the heart of the forest until I have had enough, and head towards some seats to wait for Eve.

Because of mistiming I have a 30-minute wait for Eve; it's so surprising how cold I get in that short time.

Eve arrives with a flask of hot tea, water and a towel, also some crisps: what a wonderful wife she is.

A quick cup of tea, then an even quicker walk with the dogs.

Home, and a lovely hot bath, followed by another two cups of tea, and an afternoon of dozing on the settee, listening to Radio Solent for updates on the Saints v Leeds game. I decided to give this all-ticket game a miss, after a 3-hour run I didn't fancy standing on the terraces for a couple of hours. I would then have to rush around to get to work for 18.00.

Saints win 2-0, a very good result.

Back to work and driving the water tender. We go to the General Hospital to visit a fireman from Guernsey, who is waiting to have a lung operation. He has his wife and mother and father with him, but they are genuinely pleased to see us. We spend half an hour or so chatting, and arrange to see him after the operation. We also leave a contact number if they need any help in the meantime.

CHAPTER 10

SEVEN WEEKS TO GO

"After an easy week you are now about to embark on four weeks' training which will power you to success on Marathon Day.

If you are not already running to and from work, then start to put that into your training, perhaps Tuesday and Thursday. Don't always use the same route, there might be some elite marathon runner lurking around the corner who regards you as a threat to be nibbled."

An easy week, it certainly wasn't for me.

Day 1: 3-hour walk/run

Which I'm pleased to say I did yesterday.

I intend to do yesterday's today. I wake up to the sound of the fire bells ringing. I jump out of bed and run down the stairs to the appliance room while others slide down the pole. Somebody shouts out, "Water Tender!" and the giant doors of the appliance room are thrown open. I climb into the driver's seat and rev the engine. The officer-in-charge jumps in and says, "It's a make pumps 3, Regent Street, city centre."

As I turn on the blue lights and drive out of the station, John, our acting officer-in-charge, books us mobile to the incident. They tell us that we are no longer required, but our hydraulic platform is. I reverse back into the station and one of the guys in the back jumps out to become the second man on the hydraulic platform.

Our Control comes back on the radio to tell us to go and stand by at St. Mary's fire station. I pull out of the station again: John booked us mobile with three riders due to the fact that we had to put one on the HP. Control tells us to return to the station and contact them by phone. I reverse back into the station for the second time, wondering what the hell is going on.

We phone control and they tell us to read the message again, this time properly. It said Water Tender D.56, which is Woolston, and HP D.53, which is us.

Somebody had come running down the stairs, grabbed the message and saw Water Tender and immediately thought it was ours and hence the confusion. I look at the clock and it's 3 am.

We drink tea and chat, waiting for the HP to return at 4.30 am.

I arrive home at 9.20 after a good walk in the early sunshine. Eve tells me that Kev is up in bed, he had to come back to Southampton last night to pick up some more paint and the van broke down, so his boss told him to go home and hopefully set off today.

I spend the morning generally helping Eve with dinner and reading the Sunday papers. I'm supposed to do 45 minutes of 'Enjoyable' running today; but at the moment I feel too tired, so will see how I feel later.

I don't feel any better so will give today's training a miss.

Day 2: Rest day

In running terms only, I don't stop at all today; hoovering, cooking, washing floors and even shopping. I had a guilt complex this morning about poor Eve having to do so much as well as a part-time job, so I decided to do my bit. By teatime I'm knackered. I spend the evening listening to Saints v Forest Cup replay on the radio, which Saints lose 3-1: what a day.

Day 3: 25-minute sharp run

Up at 4.15 am to see Kev off. Back to bed at 5 and stay there until 7.30 when it's up and get ready for my appointment with Bob at 9 o'clock.

A good session with Bob, I leave feeling good and fit. I decide to do my training later. Eve is working until 3 pm and I spend the time cleaning the windows inside and out. We have the rent officer coming on Thursday to look over the house, and Eve wants everything spick and span.

Every two years our landlady puts in for a rent increase, I contest it, then the rent officer comes and looks around the house, and then sets a fair rent for the next two years.

I leave to pick Eve up without doing my training. I must do it when I get back, because we are shopping tonight.

Back home and I change into my running gear. It's pouring with rain, but I decide to do tomorrow's training today, 40 minutes of fartlek.

I start off at a gentle jog until I get past the High Street, then up the pace for about a minute, and then jog slowly again. I keep this up for 40 minutes and arrive home soaking wet and exhausted. I definitely find fartlek training difficult.

While I was out, Eve phoned a London accommodation agency and booked me in for bed and breakfast on the Saturday before the marathon in Victoria.

Off shopping and catering for work, and then an evening in with a couple of cans of bitter and an *Inspector Morse* video.

Day 4: 40 minutes of fartlek

Up bright and early this morning, and looking forward to a day of birdwatching. I did today's training yesterday, so I should do a sharp 25-minute run today.

I pick Roger up at 9 o'clock and we drive out to Denny Wood, which is between Beaulieu Road and Lyndhurst. The road I ran along last Saturday.

We set off on a circular walk in bright sunshine, seeing various tits; we also see a treecreeper, a small bird that flies to the bottom of a tree, then runs up and around the tree, eating insects as it goes. But I think the highlight was when we were sitting having a cup of tea and eating sandwiches while we watched a skylark winding its way upwards while singing.

We walk a total of 7 to 8 miles spread over 4 hours; I arrive home in time for tea.

After tea I go down to the church to help clean the place up ready for our big day next Wednesday. Our new rector is being installed by the Bishop of Winchester.

There are about a dozen of us, and we spend a couple of hours removing cobwebs, polishing chairs and the brass, and generally tidying up.

I have to go there again tomorrow for a rehearsal. I'm taking part in the service as one of the representatives of the parochial church council. I don't know what I will have to do yet, but I daresay I will find out tomorrow.

I have a really full day tomorrow, including an hour's run. I think I will get up at 6.30 tomorrow morning and do the training before work.

I have a dentist's appointment during the afternoon and have an hour off work for this.

Day 5: 1-hour continuous run

I crawl out of bed at 6.20 am, put on my running gear, a modest warm-up, and out into the early morning rain. I head towards the waterfront area and do a circuit of Mayflower Park, and then the town quay. How peaceful the water looks, you could almost walk on it.

Through the city centre without a shopper in sight. Up to the Common, across the Common and home on the hour. What a great run that was. I must get up early again.

A quick bath, then off to work where I'm driving the HP. Because there is an instruction course going on, I'm detailed to ride the back of the Water Tender.

We spend the first part of the morning drilling, and after tea break the Turntable Ladder from Winchester arrives. We take it in turns to be lifted 100 feet into the air, do a complete circle and then lowered to the ground. The last time I did this was 17 years ago on my recruits' course.

I get a bit of time before dinner to wash my tunic and leggings which were still full of farmyard muck from a barn fire.

Just time to eat my dinner before we get a call to stand by at Woolston fire station. They are dealing with an incident at Vosper Thornycroft.

We are only there long enough to drink a cup of tea, but not to drink it. We eventually get back to our station at 14.10 and then that long-awaited cup of tea.

I leave work at 15.00 to drive home and pick Eve and Julie up, then to the dentist for a check-up. We all get a clean bill of health and make an appointment for a year's time.

Day 6: Rest day

Back to work this morning, and I'm detailed to drive the HP. The Water tender and HP are due to go to Fawley fire station for smoke chamber training, but for some reason our control has decided not to let the HP leave the city. After a couple of phone calls I'm told to take the HP to Fawley so that I can do my smoke and heat training.

I arrive 20 minutes after everybody else, and rush around to get my breathing apparatus set, and get to the briefing.

The briefing starts and we are told that we are called to a domestic house that is on fire. On our arrival we are told that a lot of shouting and banging had been going on before our arrival.

We are put into teams of four and three, and sent into the smoke chamber. I'm in the first team of four men, with a brief to search and rescue, and to extinguish any fires, which are indicated by an orange flashing light.

We enter the building which is full of smoke, and has a visibility that is down to zero. We search our way around a couple of rooms and find nothing. As we come to the bottom of the stairs, we find a person, or should I say a dummy, hanging from the top of the stairs. This seems to be a favourite thing lately: at the same time, we find another dummy lying on the floor. Our number one details me to take the weight of the dummy that is hanging while he cuts through the rope. The other two crew members are told to carry the other dummy.

We remove both dummies to the outside, and then return to the stairs where we meet the other team of three men. They tell us to go on a left-hand search, and they will go on a right-hand search. We should then meet with everywhere being searched.

We continue searching and make our way to the bedrooms. We meet up with the other team and they tell us that they have found a door barricaded from the outside. They knock the barricade down and force the door open, which has a wardrobe wedged against the inside. On gaining entry we find three dummies, 2 of which are child dummies laid on a bed. We bring all three dummies out while a final search is made.

We then all go to the lecture room for a debrief. We are told the scenario: a husband comes home and starts fighting with the lodger. The wife takes her two children upstairs and into a bedroom where she barricades the door with a wardrobe. The husband murders the lodger, tries to get to his wife and fails, so he barricades the door from the outside. He lights two fires on the landing, and then hangs himself.

We then have to give answers to a make-believe detective regarding what we saw and what we did, and what positions the dummies were in.

A very good drill. I felt that I had learnt something.

Back to the station in time for lunch. Both the Ladder and Water Tender disappear on a call to the General Hospital where an automatic fire alarm is sounding.

This is the time I would hate to get a shout on the HP, when I'm on my own. It's bad enough having to drive this machine, without trying to map-read and talk on the radio.

A quiet afternoon for me, and an evening of visiting both sets of parents to deliver Mother's Day presents because I won't be able to see them on Sunday.

Day 7: One hour in the park with elements of fartlek

I am going to do Sunday's big run today, and Saturday's on Sunday.

I leave home in pouring rain and high winds, to run for one and a half hours. For some reason my legs feel like lead, and I have great difficulty in keeping going. I plod on through the sports centre and Lordswood Plantation, around Chilworth, the home of the rich and famous, including Peter Shilton. Then down the Avenue towards the city, over a footbridge across the main road, then past the halls of residence of the university, onto the Common and then home.

One hour and 28 minutes, and approximately eleven miles. One of the worst runs I've done for a long time. I can only blame it on the weather.

I soak in a hot bath, then off to help Eve with some shopping. An afternoon of doing next to nothing, and listening to the Saints v Palace match on Radio Solent. I wish I hadn't bothered, they lost 2-1.

Off to work and riding BA on the back of the Ladder. What a change from driving. We have a game of indoor volleyball, and then cage operating on the HP for drill. An early supper: tonight it's 21.00 due to it being the weekend.

Just into bed when the bells go down, we have a call to smoke issuing from a takeaway on Shirley High Street.

FIREMAN ON THE RUN

Our sub-officer calls for two BA on the way to the shout, which means I have to get all my fire kit on, and breathing apparatus, before we arrive some two minutes later.

The police are already in attendance at what turns out to be a malicious false alarm.

Back to bed and a quiet night, apart from the snoring.

CHAPTER 11

SIX WEEKS TO GO

Day 1: Repeat one of your 1–1.5 runs/walks, but cut down on the walks

Luckily I did this yesterday, so today I should be doing Saturday's: one hour in the park with elements of fartlek.

I get home from work at 9.15 in time for a quick cup of tea, wash and change and off to church. This should be our last week of the interregnum, as from next Sunday Ron Diss should be with us.

During the heavy part of the service, when the vicar is blessing the bread and wine ready for Communion, a taxi driver came across the PA system asking if anybody was available for a fare at Radio Solent.

Back home from church, and Julie is cooking lunch for Mother's Day, so Eve and I sit down and read the Sunday papers. What a lovely change. We are expecting Kev home sometime today, and tomorrow he's off to Worcester.

The Sunday lunch was really lovely: Julie did an excellent job. Just as we finish, Kev arrives home looking absolutely exhausted. He's been working since 4.30 yesterday afternoon.

Eve spends the afternoon crying due to the weepy video that Julie got her to watch. I feel too tired to train, so decide to have an extra rest day.

Back to work for 18.00 and driving the water tender ladder. We have a warm-up followed by a game of volleyball. The drill night was spent tying knots blindfolded and wearing our thick, heavy gloves. All very good training, I don't have a problem tying knots blindfolded, but it is difficult feeling the line with the thick gloves.

A quiet night with no calls at all.

Day 2: 1-hour run

Arrive home at 9.20 am and manage to get Kev out of bed at 10 o'clock and his mates arrive at 11 for their journey to Worcester.

I have designed my own training programme because I have so much on and need to be flexible for the next couple of weeks.

I take Julie to college at 11.30 and then drive to the sports centre to start my 1-hour run. Another really bad run, I feel really tired and tight-chested, and at one time I thought I was going to be sick. I call it enough at 45 minutes and walk back to the car.

I hope it's just a temporary setback.

Pick Eve up from work on the way home, and decide to have a couple of hours on the allotment this afternoon putting in my onion sets.

Roger is working on his plot which is next to mine, and every half-hour we have a cup of tea and a chat, but I still manage to plant 3 lbs of onion sets, although by the time I have finished my back is aching quite a bit.

I spend the evening relaxing in front of the telly.

Day 3: 40-45 minutes of fartlek

Off to see Bob this morning: it's pouring with rain so decide to take the car. Bob spends 45 minutes working on muscle tension, and I leave feeling really good.

I drop Julie off at her friend's house, and then drive to Riverside Park to do my training. What's wrong with me? I just can't get going. I feel tired and lethargic: it's a real battle to keep going, which I lose and give up after 25 minutes.

I'm seriously thinking of seeing the doctor, but decide to wait and see how I get on on Thursday with a long run. I decide to have a rest day tomorrow, hoping this will help.

I feel ok in myself, until I start running, and then I'm just looking for a reason to stop. The worrying thing is, I'm finding them.

Home, a hot bath and something to eat; then housework. Eve is working until 3 pm today and then she is going shopping. I do the hoovering and the tidying up, feeling really sorry for myself.

I'm going down to the church this evening for the final tidy-up ready for the big service tomorrow.

Ron, who is going to be our new rector, has asked if I will wear my uniform tomorrow night. I had to get permission from my station officer, and explained that the police will be represented along with civic dignitaries. I have a small part to play alongside another member of the parochial church council.

We have to offer him bread and wine and say, "Ron be among us to break the bread and bless the cup."

Eve is busy making quiches ready for the bunfight. I must admit I'm quite looking forward to the service.

Day 4: Rest day

I spend the morning tidying up and then visiting. Firstly I go and see a fireman who is off sick and have a chat with him:

hopefully it won't be long before he is back at work. I then pop round to see my nan and spend a really pleasant hour chatting to her.

I pick Eve up from work. We arrive home and Kev's wages have come: I drive into Southampton to pay them into his account.

I'm also trying to buy a two-bar electric fire for my nan, but not had any luck: you can buy all the fancy fires, but not the old two-bar sort.

I'm still not feeling right, my legs ache and so does my head: I'm pleased that it's a rest day. Eve has been very busy all afternoon making quiches and sausage rolls for this evening.

I have to go to the station to collect my uniform.

We leave home just after 6 to deliver the food to the school hall where the reception is being held. The tables are already quite full of food and it's beginning to look lovely.

We have to be in church early as Eve is a sidesperson and is needed to show people to their seats and generally help out.

The service starts at 7.30 pm, but by 7.15 people are standing. We must have between four and five hundred people in church, including 40 vicars who have all come to support Ron in his new parish.

The Bishop of Winchester pays a very respectful opening address to Ron, and the service lasts about an hour.

My small part goes well, so I'm pleased to say the whole thing was a complete success. We all leave church to walk to the school hall for the reception, where I find Joan, a member of the choir, wearing a hearing aid. I didn't realise that she was deaf. She soon points out to me that she's not:

she was listening to Radio Solent for the Saints v Man Utd game, which ended up as a 1-1 draw.

We spend a pleasant hour talking to people from Ron's old parish of Maybush and we all agree it's our gain and their loss.

Day 5: 2-3-hour run/walk

A bad night of feeling sick and generally unwell. I eventually get out of bed about 9 am and decide that I'm in no fit state to go running. I drop Julie at college and then do the catering for work. Everything is an effort.

Eve arrives home from work and we both have a snack, then decide to take the dogs for a walk. It was an effort at first, but became enjoyable as we plodded on through the middle of the Plantation doing a circular walk of 3-4 miles.

When we get home, both the dogs need a good wash, and I spend an hour sitting down and feeling sorry for myself.

Eve is convinced that I have a sinus infection, and goes to the chemist to get me a course of Dimotapp to see if that will help. I'm feeling really frustrated not doing my training, although the training programme says not to train if feeling unwell.

I'm due back at work tomorrow, but will see how I feel in the morning.

Day 6: 45-minute run

Up bright and early and get ready for work. I feel a bit better this morning but still very tired. I drop Eve off at work just before 8.30 and then stop to buy some vegetables for the meal at work.

Driving the HP today, we spend the first part of the morning on the drill yard. After running up the 50-foot ladder, I reach the top and feel totally exhausted. Someone said that they had seen their doctor suffering from the same symptoms as me, and were told that there was a virus doing the rounds.

During the middle of the drill the Water Tender had a call to a car leaking petrol.

After tea break we spend time doing maintenance on the equipment and general cleaning. Lunchtime and we just start eating, when the bells go down. Both pumps are sent to the General Hospital for a smell of burning. I am left on the station alone, and spend my lunch hour answering the telephone.

Back on the drill yard for more drills after lunch, and then down the local park for a warm-up and a game of football. We play for 30 minutes, and I do a good bit of running around and don't feel too bad.

Home and an evening in front of the telly, and hopefully feeling fitter tomorrow.

Day 7: Rest day

Another rest day today, hopefully it will do me some good: I'm definitely feeling better.

Driving the Water Tender today, we spend the morning drilling and physical training which includes 30 minutes of football and then cleaning. Every Saturday morning the appliance room floor is scrubbed and polished.

Time for lunch, an early one today, as this afternoon we are going to a school fête with Welephant. After he got attacked by some drunken yobs, he's not allowed to be left alone.

Welephant is a red elephant that goes around promoting fire safety to children at schools and fêtes.

Today we had a spare man to put on the suit. But sometimes one of the crew has to do it, and it gets quite funny if we pick up a call, and passers-by see this red elephant rolling about in the back of the fire engine trying to get changed.

Saints lose 4-3 at home to Everton and are now dangerously close to relegation. I spend a quiet evening in front of the telly, hoping that I'll be ok tomorrow for the Eastleigh 10k road race.

CHAPTER 12

FIVE WEEKS TO GO

Day 1: Eastleigh 10k road race

Off to church this morning, our first service with our new rector. There are a lot more people in church than normal, all coming to see Ron for the first time, I expect.

Back home for lunch, I sit eating a ham roll while Eve and Julie tuck into a Sunday roast. I feel quite good and decide to take part in the run. I feel really nervous, but it is the first race I have done in nearly three years.

We arrive in Eastleigh just after 14.00 with the start of the race at 14.30. I spend 10 minutes stretching and warming up; I take my place towards the back and on the outside of the 1200 runners; I don't want to get caught up in the main pack, as you tend to go off too fast.

The gun fires and off we go. The very good and the very foolish shoot off at a 5-minute-mile pace while I plod on at my comfortable 8-minute-mile pace. The sun is shining and the conditions are perfect. I feel myself being pulled along at a faster pace, I slow up a bit and realise how easy it is to go at a faster pace than I want to.

The atmosphere is great: everybody is laughing and joking and generally jockeying for a position where you have room to manoeuvre.

At the 2k point we come to the only real hill. I notice that some of the people who sprinted off at the beginning are now walking up the hill. I manage the hill quite easily and feel really good.

A long, downhill stretch and I pass the halfway stage where there is a marshal calling the time: as I pass he calls out 25 minutes exactly, a bit slower than I thought but feeling good, so I up the pace slowly. We are kept to the right as we pass the finish line for the first time at 6k, the course goes on another 4k and brings us back to the finish line, where we enter on the left this time. I cross the line with a time of 48 minutes 50 seconds.

As we are marshalled through we are all given a medal, a cold drink and various application forms for future 10k road races in the area.

Back home and a belated Sunday roast, and then off to work. Riding BA on the Water Tender ladder, and a very quiet evening. I'm kitchen man tonight and cook a ham omelette for supper.

Day 2: 50-60-minute run

A quiet night, and up to cook a breakfast for eight firemen. We just finish breakfast and the Water Tender gets a call that turns out to be malicious.

I leave the station after a good warm-up and run towards the sports centre, through the sports centre and up a long, uphill stretch past the golf club and down a short hill. It's then up this really steep hill leading to a footbridge across the main road, which I admit I walk up and over. Then carry on running past the halls of residence for the university and into the Common; through the Common and out onto the road with a mile to go before reaching home.

Exactly an hour. I feel quite good at the end, which is a big confidence booster after last week.

Kev is still in bed, so I get him up so that he is ready to leave at midday. He's off to Redditch today for seven days.

I pick Eve up from work, then spend an hour on the allotment drinking tea and talking to Roger.

Home for tea and then off to work where I'm driving the HP. A quiet evening for me cooking the supper.

Day 3: 30-35 minutes of sharp fartlek

Home by 9.30 and I feel knackered, but the thought of 12 days off seems great. I'm unable to fit a run in today, but I'm not too worried, because the rest ready for Friday and a 20-mile run won't hurt.

Bob is having a day off today so no Alexander Technique. I spend the morning talking to Julie who is off college through illness.

After lunch I drive to Eastleigh to my parents to fix a loose tap, only a slight success, but it should hold until the plumber arrives. Then I visit my grandmother and deliver an electric fire that she asked me to get for her and repair a plug.

Budget Day today, nothing really surprising except the reduction in poll tax. I attend a meeting in the evening of the church council where we discuss services during Easter Week, and discuss and prepare for our AGM in April.

Day 4: Short 30-minute run

Eve has taken today off and Julie is still off college. I decide to go out for my run this morning, which feels really good, and I have to force myself to keep to only 30 minutes.

Shopping after lunch, we drive to our local supermarket and do battle with everybody else for 60 minutes. Wouldn't it be good and cheaper if we didn't have to eat? We bump into Tracy, Roger's wife, and give her a lift home. A quick cup of tea, and Roger and I arrange to go birdwatching at 8 o'clock tomorrow morning at Pagham near Chichester.

Day 5: Rest day

I pick Roger up at 8, and we drive to Pagham Harbour which is east of Chichester. We arrive about 9 o'clock and set off to walk around one side of the harbour during the morning and try to do the other side during the afternoon.

We take our sandwiches and flasks and stop at the first hide we come to and have our first of many cups of tea: we had only been walking for five minutes.

The hide looks across a road to a pond: the only problem is that every time a lorry goes by our vision is blocked.

After 30 minutes or so, we walk along a very muddy footpath, where we get a very good look at a yellowhammer. We then hear the beautiful singing of a lark and watch him circling above us.

We carry on walking for about an hour and a half, the cut through a churchyard where we see a red-legged partridge walking along a boundary wall. Into another hide for tea and sandwiches where we sit for an hour looking at various species across the harbour.

We walk back to the car for a new flask of tea and more sandwiches which we load into our bags, and set off around the other side of the harbour. We walk along country lanes, across fields that are full of sheep and lambs. It's so peaceful; we just stop and watch the lambs trying to find their mothers. Whenever the lambs try and feed from the wrong sheep they are nudged out of the way until they find their own mother.

On to the sea wall for about a mile, then through another field, and we are finally around the other side of the harbour, where we stop for tea and sandwiches.

I feel a bit concerned because my back is beginning to play up and we are about three miles from the car.

We make our way back to the car with a stop for more tea, and eventually arrive back at 5.30 pm. We have been out for eight and a half hours and have seen 51 different species of birds.

As we drive back to Southampton I can feel my back stiffening up and I begin to wonder if I have done too much, with a 20-mile run to do tomorrow.

Day 6: 20-mile run

I decide to treat today's run as a complete rehearsal for the big day. I get up early and feel good, not too stiff after yesterday's walking marathon. A slice of toast and a cup of tea, a quick read of the paper followed by a good warm-up. I set my stopwatch and make sure that I have a piece of chalk. I have agreed to write my initials on the pavement at a certain point.

Mike, a friend and colleague, is going to ride his bike alongside me once I get close to where he lives. The idea is that if I get to the rendezvous point and he's not there, I will write my initials on the pavement, he will then know that I have gone past and he can ride and catch me up.

I leave home at 10 past 9 and set off at a steady pace towards Totton where I'm due to meet Mike at 9.30. The sun is shining, but a cold wind blows off the river as I cross the causeway. I can see Mike waiting at the top of the hill. I meet him dead on time, and notice that I'm right on course for an 8-minute-mile pace.

We carry on up the hill through Hounsdown and towards Ashurst. On through Ashurst towards the capital of the New Forest, Lyndhurst. I take my first drink of water that Mike is carrying for me at Ashurst Bridge, and push on into Lyndhurst which is about 9 miles into the run.

We now turn into the heart of the Forest and head towards Beaulieu Road. I feel pretty good but notice some of the hills are becoming a struggle.

Beaulieu Road and 13 miles done. It's really nice to have someone to talk to while running. It definitely takes my mind off the aches and pains developing in my hips.

Mike produces a carton of fresh orange juice, which I drink while running; he also offers a great deal of encouragement as we approach the 18-mile mark at Marchwood. Two miles to go and it's becoming a struggle to keep going. I plod on and complete the 20 miles in under 3 hours. How much under three hours I don't know, because I forgot to get Mike to stop the watch, or to note the time when we finished. It's only when we are in his car and heading towards home, that I notice the time is 10 past 12. I imagine my time would have been around 2 hours 50 minutes.

Home, a hot bath, and lots of cold drinks. The lunchtime post arrives with further details of the London Marathon regarding registration etc.

I spend the rest of the afternoon and evening pottering about.

Day 7: Rest day

A lie-in this morning, and a bit of a struggle to get out of bed, my hips are quite sore, but pleased that my back is feeling good.

Eve is out shopping, Julie is at work and Kevin is still travelling back from Redditch; so I decide to have a good fried breakfast which I really enjoy. I clean and wash all the evidence up before Eve gets home, and then leave for the church at 10 o'clock where we are attempting to put the cross back in position after repairs and painting.

Although the sun is shining, it's bitterly cold. I'm the first to arrive, so unlock the church and get things ready. To get the cross back in place involves three men 100 feet up in the bell tower pulling on ropes and shackles to stop the cross crashing into the church, and one man stands on the island in the centre of the road with his arms outstretched like wings, directing those above on the level of the cross as it is hauled aloft.

This is a very busy road, and you can imagine the comments and stares as people drive past to see a grown man standing in the middle of the road pretending to be an aeroplane.

Three hours and three attempts later, the cross is back in place, shining out as a beacon to the people of Freemantle.

I arrive home cold and hungry, and spend the afternoon listening to the Chelsea v Saints game on the radio which Saints win 2-0.

Kev is home, but sound asleep, so I haven't spoken to him yet. Eve asks if I enjoyed my fried breakfast.

A nice quiet evening. Kev gets up and goes out for a pint or two.

CHAPTER 13

FOUR WEEKS TO GO

Day 1: Maybe this is your half-marathon

There should only be one in your whole training programmes. Oh well, that is what the training programme states: hopefully I haven't messed things up by running more.

I'm back onto the programme again after spending a couple of weeks doing my own thing. I had decided to have three rest days after Friday's big run.

Eve and myself decide to go to church together: today is Palm Sunday and we take part in the procession through and around the church carrying our palm crosses.

Home and a rush around to cook the Sunday dinner and get tidied up. Today we are off to Roger's house for Patrick's first birthday party. I spend a couple of hours playing with all the children and organising games. I don't think I have ever grown up.

We leave Roger's at 6.30 and are only home for ten minutes, when Eve's brother, Ron, and family turn up unexpectedly.

Ron and I disappear for a couple of hours down the local and leave Eve, Ann and the two boys playing. Five pints later we arrive home, and Ann and Ron leave.

Day 2: Rest day

A quick tidy-up during the morning, then it's off to Roger's and then to the allotment with all our potatoes ready for planting. The sun is shining, but a cold wind is blowing. A new fence is being put up around the allotments; I have agreed to let the men borrow my shed to keep their tools in. What a mistake: I can't get in because of the amount of stuff they have stored there.

I eventually find my spade; one of the fencers was using it. I must admit I wasn't too polite in telling them what I thought.

I plant 14 lbs of early potatoes amid considerable amounts of tea. I think we upset a few of the old boys by spending a lot of time sitting in our chairs drinking tea, and putting the world to rights. They think that you are there to dig and re-dig your plot. Home, and an aching back due to all the bending. An easy evening, apart from picking Julie up later on.

Day 3: 60–70-minute run

I get up bright and early and set off towards the Common. A fine drizzle and bitterly cold: what a difference from yesterday.

I feel really good and start thinking about the marathon and wish it was today, because I feel really fit and good. I think the three rest days must have really helped.

I head on through the Common, past the university, and then past the halls of residence, out onto the Avenue and across the footbridge and down to the golf course.

I remember my one and only attempt at golf; that was just after Kev was born, when I had a game with Ron, my brother-in-law, who plays off a handicap of eight. I did the classic, I hit the ball eventually, it flew straight and hit a tree and bounced back behind me.

I push on past the golf course and into the sports centre and out onto the road and eventually home.

A quick bath and then off to see Bob Donovan for more

relaxation and posture exercises. I spend 45 minutes with Bob and leave as usual feeling totally relaxed and free of tension.

I pick Eve up from work on the way home, and an afternoon of generally tidying up the garden, and giving the newly turfed lawn its first cut. It seems to have taken really well.

Kevin arrives home unexpectedly from London where he's working. They were unable to find a bed and breakfast, so having a night at home and leaving at 4 am tomorrow to travel back to London.

Day 4: An extra rest day

I first get up at 3.30 am to give Kev a call, and then back to bed. Eve brings me a cup of tea at 8 o'clock, and I eventually get up at 8.30.

A general tidy-up, then I make a casserole for tonight's dinner.

Off to the allotment at midday and I spend the afternoon drinking tea and planting peas, beetroot, carrots, and radishes. The chaps doing the fence are still here, but reckon they will finish tomorrow. It will be nice to get my shed back to normal.

It's another beautiful day: very relaxing to be working on the allotment with the sounds of birds for company.

A quiet evening watching the England v Ireland match on TV, which ended in a 1-1 boring draw.

Day 5: 70-90 minutes of running

A busy day today, so decided to do the run as early as possible. The sun is shining and I'm feeling good and set off on my

10-mile route. I head towards the Plantation, out the other side, and past the big houses of Chilworth. I'm feeling so good I decide to make this my big run of the week, so take in an extra 3-mile loop, bringing me past the golf course and back through the Plantation, then out through Chilworth once again. Down the Avenue and across the footbridge, which takes me down towards the university, then into the Common, then eventually home on the 2-hour mark.

A hot bath, a bit of hoovering and tidying up, then down to the allotment to sow various seeds, drink tea and put the world to rights with Roger.

Home in time for tea, and then off to church for a Communion service, followed by Stripping of the Altar, a ceremony which takes place on Maundy Thursday. Everything is removed from the altar to leave just the wooden table with no cross or coverings.

An early night and I even manage to finish my library book.

Day 6: Rest day

Up bright and early and off to Eastleigh with Eve. We first go to the cemetery to place flowers on her brother's grave. It would have been his birthday today. It doesn't seem possible that he died three years ago. We were at our neighbour's funeral: as we arrived back indoors the phone was ringing, it was Eve's other brother telling us that Ern had died.

Ern was only 35 when he died. It just seems such a waste. He was a smashing chap who would do anything for anyone.

We leave the cemetery and drive to my grandmother's house to give her a bunch of flowers for Easter, and a good old chat.

An hour later we call on my sister-in-law: I spend an hour playing football, golf, cricket, chase and finally a good old free-for-all with my two nephews, David and Andrew.

It's then off to my parents to spend a couple of hours gardening and planting onion sets. It's nice to see my dad getting about in his electric wheelchair.

Home, and I pop down the road to a disabled neighbour and repair her washing line. Home in time for tea and an evening in front of the TV.

Day 7: 1 Hour easy but with a varied pace

Eve leaves home early to do some shopping, while I make the sandwiches and get things ready for our day out.

We are going to the Meon Valley to do one of the walks featured in the local newspaper. We have chosen a 6.5-mile circular walk, starting at a village called Charlton, close to Denmead and Corhampton.

The sun is shining when we leave the car for a really steep uphill climb. We get to the top where there is a windmill: that's probably why it is called Windmill Hill. The windmill has had various extensions built on, and it's now a residential home.

We walk on, up and down various hills with beautiful views across the Meon Valley; along deserted lanes, and across open fields. Eventually stopping to eat our sandwiches in a quiet corner of a field.

We are passed by occasional people who are also doing the walk, but in the main we see nobody.

After lunch we set off for a steep uphill climb with views

into Sussex, then finally a long downhill stretch back to the car.

We were walking for about 4 hours and have both caught the sun on our faces.

Home in time to hear the football results: Saints drew 3-3 away to Manchester City.

A relaxing evening ready to go back to work tomorrow.

CHAPTER 14

THREE WEEKS TO GO

Day 1: Your Last Opportunity for a Half-Marathon
If not, then spend lots of lovely time in the country,
running/walking 3-6 hours.

Well, I did the half-marathon distance on Thursday, and the long run last Friday. This means I should be doing something like an hour's run. But what with the clocks going forward, being at work and having visitors during the evening, I have found the perfect excuse for doing nothing.

Back to work on days, and driving the Ladders, I'm also duty cook, so spend the morning cooking a roast dinner for 8. I also make a curry for tomorrow's meal.

Just after lunch we get a call to a fire in a house which turns out to be a malicious false alarm. I wonder if the people who make these calls realise the consequences of doing this.

Only this week two young children were killed after being involved in an accident with a fire appliance responding to a malicious call.

We arrive back to the station to get changed, and then off to the hospital, so that I can deliver a basket of fruit to a Dorset fireman who has just had a heart bypass operation.

We then paint and check a few hydrants, then change again ready for sport. We drive down to the local park for a good warm-up followed by 35 minutes of football. This is the only running I have done today. I must make sure I don't let myself down during these last three weeks before the marathon.

I walk home from work: Eve's mum and dad are down for tea. I then run them home in the car later that evening.

Day 2: Rest day

Driving the Hydraulic Platform today, as it's a Bank Holiday we are allowed to stand down for the day, which means apart from checking equipment we can do as we wish, as long as we remain ready for any incident.

We have the curry today that I made yesterday, so there is nothing to do in the kitchen until lunchtime.

I spend the morning washing and polishing the car, as I do every Bank Holiday. We have a busy morning with 5 calls, but none of them of any consequence.

We get a call from our control room telling us to send a leading fireman to the local hospital with a ring cutter to remove a ring from a male person. When we arrive we are taken to an operating theatre where a gentleman is lying on the operating table with a ball race wedged over his manhood. Apparently he has been in this position for the last five hours.

It took a further hour with six firemen and an operating team using an angled cutting disk to remove the object, and not a drop of blood was spilt.

After lunch I finish off the car, spend half an hour in the gym doing mainly stretches. I then shower, then sit down to watch the first half of Saints v Liverpool on the TV.

I rush home during half-time to watch the second half of the match which Saints win 1-0.

During the evening I pick Julie up from Bitterne and watch the James Bond film.

Day 3: 60-minute run

Up bright and early this morning, Kevin left for London at 5.30 am. I got up two hours later to generally get in Eve's way. It's her first day of full-time work today, it will seem strange not having her home in the afternoons.

Off to see Bob Donovan this morning, he informs me that my head is not straight on my shoulders. He spends time working on my neck and shoulder muscles, and then on my legs which are still very tense, especially my hamstrings. I leave him 45 minutes later feeling good, and with my head now straight, to drive home. Get changed ready for my training run.

I'm going to change this week's training around a bit, so that I can tie it in with my nights. I intend to do next Sunday's big run this Friday, with Mike from work riding his bike alongside me again.

I leave home in very windy and rainy conditions. I run past the rectory and see Ron busy at his desk in the window. He gives me a wave and I push on past the church, then up to The Dell where they are taking down TV cameras from yesterday.

Past The Dell and onwards towards the Common, then out towards the university. I'm feeling good so decide that I will keep running for 70-90 minutes which is supposed to be Thursday's run.

On past the university, past the halls of residence, out onto the Avenue, over the footbridge and into the Chilworth area of Southampton; past all the mansions and big houses of Chilworth, then into the small village itself. Through the Plantation, past the hospital where I think I wish the surgeon who did my back operation could see me now. I would like to shake his hand, and remind him that I told him that I would work and run again.

Home with exactly 90 minutes on the watch. I must get my watch strap fixed before the marathon.

A hot soak in the bath, something to eat, then a bit of housework and prepare the meal, before picking up Miss Cave from the corner shop to take her for a physiotherapy appointment at the General Hospital.

Back from the hospital, dish up the dinner that Julie cooked; Eve arrives home from work closely followed by Kev.

Off to work and fifth man on the back of the Water Tender. A quiet evening and bed at midnight.

Day 4: 30–40 minutes of fartlek

Only in bed for 30 minutes and we get a call to the maternity hospital. As we approach the hospital we can see clouds of smoke, but getting closer we notice a large bonfire in a garden, which is possibly the cause of our call.

We book in at the hospital to find that they called us because they could smell smoke, which on checking was coming from the bonfire.

Our sub-officer sends our crew to have a word with the people, and to check that everything was under control. Which it was: the young couple who were having the bonfire were asked why they were having one so late. They explained that they had waited for everyone to take their washing in.

Back to bed about 1.30 am and I lay there until 7 o'clock. I help cook the breakfast, then a general tidy-up before going off duty. I get changed into running gear and leave the station for an hour's run.

I head off through the estate, over a road bridge and out to Eling; then around the creek into Totton. Through the precinct to Testwood, across the boardwalk by the River Test, and back through the estate to the fire station to collect my uniform and car.

Home and a soak in the bath, then get stuck into the housework. Julie is on a split shift in her part-time job, coming home at 1 o'clock and then going back at 4 pm. I spend an hour sitting down talking, then do a bit of ironing and preparing the evening meal.

Eve comes in from work at 5.15 and I leave at 5.30.

17.59 Duty Watch parade. I'm detailed to drive the Water Tender. We check the equipment, then drive to the park for a game of football.

During the evening we pick up a call to a fire in a house in Portswood. I really enjoy the drive, but the fire turns out to be nothing.

Day 5: 70-90-minute run

I did this run on Tuesday, so today is going to be a rest day ready for my big run tomorrow.

We get tipped out of bed at 4 am to deal with a car leaking petrol, this takes an hour before we get back to bed.

Home just after 9 o'clock and four days off.

Another day of housework and dozing in the chair. I wanted to get down to my allotment, but the weather is too bad.

I spend a bit of time reading through my Marathon details regarding registration, and getting to the start etc. it makes me feel a bit nervous, and I wonder if I'm capable of finishing.

No meal to prepare today: Kevin is buying us a meal from the chippy. Julie had hers at lunchtime because she is working from 4 to 7. Eve gets home just after 5, followed by Kev.

Day 6: Rest day

I wake up feeling really tired and stiff, and to think today I'm doing a half-marathon followed by a 4-mile walk.

I have two slices of toast for breakfast, then change into my running gear. Mike Gass is going to pick me up: we will drive to Totton, do the run, then I will walk home from Eling.

I spend a good 15 minutes warming up and trying to get rid of the stiffness. I know that today is really going to be a struggle.

Mike arrives right on time and we drive to the start of the half-marathon course. I set off on my own, while Mike takes his car home and gets his bike. He rides to meet me three miles into the run.

A very strong wind is blowing, and it's very overcast as I leave the car. I find it a real struggle to get going, also feeling really stiff again after spending time sitting in the car. I even consider stopping and going back home. I think I would have if Mike was with me instead of getting his bike.

I meet Mike three miles into the run. I'm feeling a bit better, and into my running action. Once I start chatting, the tiredness leaves me. I begin to relax a bit more and push on towards the countryside and off the main road.

A very strong wind blowing directly into our faces really makes the going difficult; I only hope that we don't get these conditions on the big day. I push on and reach the finish, approximately 14 miles, in 1 hour 56 minutes. Quite a slow time, but I'm quite pleased due to the conditions. I slip on a tracksuit, and set off for the 4-mile walk home which takes another 1 hour and 5 minutes. Giving me a total of three hours and 5 minutes; my last really big session now completed. I just wish I felt more confident.

I spend the afternoon shopping and tidying up, and an evening in front of the telly feeling exhausted.

Day 7: One hour enjoyable in the park

I managed this session on Wednesday, so all I have to do is a 45-minute fartlek session. Eve leaves home early to do her shopping while I tidy up. We decide to take the dogs out for a walk at Farley Mount near Winchester. The wind is really blowing but we spend an hour walking and playing with the dogs, which I'm going to treat as today's run.

Home to listen to the National, which doesn't make us rich, and Saints match away to Tottenham.

I remember a couple of seasons ago when I went with Mike Curtis to White Hart Lane to watch Saints and Spurs in an FA Cup match.

We had paid £10 for the seat, only to have a policeman stand directly in front of us. After complaining to no avail, things got a bit heated: a chap sitting near me stood up and told everybody to calm down. He was immediately arrested and then things got really heated. At one stage I was being lifted out of my seat by two policemen. I was being arrested for complaining bitterly about the policeman who was causing all the problems.

Luckily a police inspector had been watching all this from another part of the ground. He came to tell the officers trying to arrest me to leave me alone, and assured me that he would be dealing with the policeman causing the trouble.

I did make an official complaint, which I eventually dropped, after being assured by a senior officer on the telephone that internal discipline was taking place.

Saints won that game, but I'm sorry to say that they lost 2-0 today.

An evening of relaxing with Eve. Oh, guess what? I had a new strap fitted to my watch yesterday, so no more fishing in my pocket for my watch.

CHAPTER 15

TWO WEEKS TO GO

Day 1: How long do you estimate the Marathon will take you?
3 hours, 3.5, 4, 4.5. Take your map which you will be familiar with, and run/walk for two-thirds of your estimated marathon time. It is best to do a circular route from home with the possibility of taking some short cuts.

Well, I hope to finish within four and a half hours, so I did my three hours of training last Friday. Today is going to be a rest day. I get out of bed at 8.30 and get ready for church. Eve is not feeling that good, so I'm off to church on my own.

The first thing I see when I arrive is the parish magazine with a picture of the start of the London Marathon on the front cover. I feel quite guilty because more than one person came up to me and talked about the Marathon, and asked what charity I was running for, or did I have a sponsor form?

I had to explain that, due to my back operation, I have to take each day as it comes, and I haven't really known if I was capable of even finishing the London Marathon. I explained that if I had agreed to run for a charity, I would be putting more pressure on myself to finish.

I think I will have a word with the rector and ask him to mention this to the congregation, and perhaps instead of sponsorship, they would like to make a donation to the church if I manage to finish.

Home from church, and I give Eve a hand with the roast. Kev is away in London but should be home tonight when his contract finishes, so he will be back on the dole from tomorrow.

We drive up to see Eve's parents after lunch, and see her dad, whose birthday it is today. Ron, Eve's brother, and his wife Ann and the two boys are also there. They tell me that they will be travelling up to London to watch the Marathon. I will have quite a gathering cheering me on.

The doubts about finishing are certainly on my mind. I have to keep telling myself that I'm perfectly capable of running the distance.

I spend the evening reading the paper and watching the TV.

Day 2: Rest day

Back on duty today. I call at the veg shop on the way to work to pick up some fresh vegetables.

BA on the back of the Water Tender Ladder. We spend the whole morning drilling in the yard, and by lunchtime I feel quite tired.

We have a new probationer join us today, that makes four; I remember when we were a watch with experience. But we are now a Watch with a third of the Watch having less than two years' experience.

It certainly puts pressure on the older men. Also I don't think it's fair on the new lads to be grouped together like this without some fire-fighting experience first. You could get the situation where two probationers could be going into their very first major fire together. Talk about the blind leading the blind.

A peaceful lunchtime and an afternoon of hydrant maintenance and physical training. For the latter we have 45 minutes of football down the local park.

Home and a run to be done, due to the fact that tomorrow I will not have any spare time to fit in a 40-minute run, unless I do it at 6 am tomorrow morning.

I decide to do an hour's run tonight, what with the 45 minutes of football already done, this will give me the 90 minutes that I need to do.

I leave home and head towards the city centre, and then run past the pier. You can still see the damage from a fire there 3 or so years ago. On towards Ocean Village, and past where the old floating bridge used to be, with the new Itchen Bridge towering above.

When the bridge was first built, the council said that they would only charge a toll until they had raised enough money to pay for the bridge. All I can say is that it must have cost millions.

Under the bridge and along the backroads towards Northam, across a level crossing footbridge. I always seem to time it wrong: the barriers are down waiting for a train. Back into the city, and then home with 59 minutes on the watch.

Kev has bought himself a new stereo with a remote control: I spend an hour reading the **instructions** and still none the wiser. Midnight, and bed: I'm glad that I don't have to get up at 6 am to do the run.

Day 3: 90-minute run

I managed to do this yesterday, so today now becomes a rest day. A pleasant walk to work to blow the cobwebs away. BA on the Water Tender. I must say this is a pleasant change from driving.

We have a lecture all morning from a fire prevention officer on how to carry out an inspection on a rest home. It's very difficult to stay awake, not because it's boring, but because we are sitting in armchairs in a warm, smokey restroom. Our lecture room is being used by the recruits' course.

Another peaceful lunch hour; then an afternoon of drill in the yard and football.

A very quiet couple of days, I hope this doesn't mean we are in for a couple of rough nights.

I walk home from work, and then off to the AGM of the parochial church council. I'm re-elected for another year. I eventually have my tea at 9.30 and hear on the radio that the Saints drew 1-1 with Arsenal at The Dell.

Day 4: Rest day

It should be an extra rest day today, but I will have to do tomorrow's run today. A 75-100-minute run. The way I feel, I would have a job to run 75 to 100 yards – sorry, I should say metres. As I leave home I really find it a struggle; my legs feel like lead weights. I feel fine in myself, but just not right for running.

I plod on towards the sports centre and a long, uphill struggle into the Plantation. I still feel like turning around and heading for home, but I manage to win the psychological battle and push on out onto the road and through Chilworth, along the Avenue towards the city, all downhill now, but still a struggle. I eventually arrive home 75 minutes after leaving.

I spend an hour giving Kev a hand to programme in his new stereo. It's like a computer: it even says hello when you turn it on.

Off to see the doctor for a blood pressure check: great news, it's the best it's ever been, 120 over 70. The doctor asks if I'm running again. I explain all about the training programme and ask if I'm ok to run the Marathon. He said I'm not only ok to run, I also stand a chance of winning. Well, finishing anyway.

Off to work at 18.00 and I'm driving the HP. What a blessing: the other two appliances are in and out all night, including going to a fire near Winchester. I wonder why nights are getting so busy?

Day 5: 75-100-minute run

I'm pleased to say I did this yesterday. Today I'm going to do tomorrow's 45-minute run. It really seems complicated: I'm not sure if today is yesterday or tomorrow.

Up out of bed at 7 am and feeling totally exhausted. I help cook breakfast, then a pleasant stroll home.

I check on two elderly neighbours before going indoors to get changed for a couple of hours' work on the allotment, planting parsnips, and generally tidying up. Spring has truly sprung: there are more people than normal, all busy on their plots. It seems so peaceful, planting and listening to the birds singing.

I feel really tired now, so head for home to make a steak and kidney pie for tea, a little housework, and doze in the chair. Then it's back to work and driving the Water Tender Ladder.

We start the shift by playing football for 45 minutes, which is exactly my training time.

A first aid lecture. It seems really strange that we are not qualified first-aiders. The service will not pay for you to take a first aid certificate once you have left training school.

Midnight and to a long-awaited bed.

Day 6: Rest day

A quiet night and home just after 9am. I spend most of the morning installing a telephone extension in our bedroom; I'm surprised that it actually works.

A bit of housework, tidying and hoovering three bedrooms, stairs and hallway. Cook a meal, and also fix a new washing line for a disabled lady down the road.

I'll never understand the amount of work carried out by a housewife.

I could spend hours talking to the disabled lady down the road: she used to live the life of a Romany, and some of the stories she tells me are fascinating. She wrote a very brief article for the parish magazine all about her childhood days. It was excellent reading. It's only recently that she has lost both legs due to an illness. She never moans and is a real example to the rest of us.

A very relaxing evening and an early night.

Day 7: 45 minutes of enjoyable running in the park

I did this on Thursday, so I'm doing tomorrow's run today. A pleasant country run of 75-90 minutes.

I get out of bed at 8.30 am feeling fit and relaxed, but whenever I think of next Sunday, the butterflies in my stomach start flapping.

A light breakfast of tea and toast, followed by a good warm-up, and then off on my last big run.

I run along the cycle path towards Totton: the sun is really shining, and I'm soon breaking into a sweat.

I turn off the main road and head into the countryside around Nursling. As I pass the River Test, Green Watch from my station are drilling on the bridge, setting hoses into the river. We exchange some rude comments and I push on into Nursling and the open countryside, past Northcliffe School, which is a large boarding school. Out onto the main road, past Romsey golf course, past my favourite pub where we'll be tonight with friends Mike and June. Through the Millbrook Estate, and home with 1 hour 25 minutes on the watch.

A long, hot soak, then my pre-match meal of pizza and beans, before going off to The Dell to watch Saints v Sunderland.

My dad is from Sunderland, and it's such a shame that both clubs are at the bottom of the First Division fighting for survival. If we win today we will be safe, but poor Sunderland will be in serious trouble.

A typical relegation battle, which we win 3-1 and are now safe in the First Division. We spend the evening out with Mike and June. I drink too much bitter. I intend not to have another drink now until after the Marathon. I wonder if I will succeed?

CHAPTER 16

ONE WEEK TO GO, MARATHON WEEK

Day 1: A pleasant run of 75-90 minutes

Well, I did that yesterday, so today becomes a rest day.

Off to church this morning and Ron our rector tells everybody about the Marathon next week, and that I will be running. A lot of people come up and wish me well after the service. They also tell me that they will say a prayer for me. I think I will need as many of these as I can get, and I will certainly be saying one.

Home from church, and I volunteer to hoover the lounge, so that I can watch the semi-final of the FA Cup between Spurs and Arsenal. Later the other semi-final between Nottingham Forest and West Ham will also be shown.

Spurs beat Arsenal 3-1, and Forest beat West Ham 4-0: what a cracking final this should make.

I spend half an hour listing the things I want to take to London with me, and also reading through the training guide. I have two short runs to do this week, one of 20 minutes and the other 30 minutes.

The guide stresses the importance of mental preparation, and gives various tips and relaxation techniques.

Eve has worked out a daily menu to increase carbohydrates. I have taken Friday night off work this week, which will hopefully guarantee me a good night's sleep before travelling to London on Saturday and a restless night in a strange bed.

Day 2: Rest day

An early start today. I have to do the catering for work, and various other bits and pieces this morning. I fly around Sainsbury's, then take all the food to the fire station. The Duty Watch are out drilling and I have a quick cup of tea with Pam the station cook.

Into Shirley to draw some money out of the bank, then back home to get Kev up: he's travelling to London this afternoon for a night's work. Julie comes home from college during her lunch break; she's indoors for 20 minutes, and then gone again.

I manage to sit down for 20 minutes during the afternoon to mentally prepare for Sunday. They recommend that you think your run through, and plan how you intend to run it. My plan is to start at a very easy 8-9-minute-mile pace, and then try to maintain an 8-minute pace for as long as I can. I have no intention of trying to break any records, I just want to finish somewhen on Sunday.

I was talking to a neighbour today about the Marathon, he wished be luck and said he hoped that I would win it. I just hope he doesn't put any money on me.

A quiet evening apart from picking Julie up.

Day 3: A sharpish (not too sharpish) run of 30 minutes

Back to work today and driving the Water Tender. I have an hour off, to buy catering: I have been asked to cater for 40 teenagers who are coming to the station tomorrow night for a quiz.

Back in time to take part in a drill session to help a probationer prepare for his probationary practical exam this afternoon. We run through some of the drills that we think he may get.

Time for lunch – well, only just. We pick up a call to a lockout. Back to the station to make a cup of tea, we don't get time to drink it, as we get a call to an automatic fire alarm operating at a local supermarket. Back to the station and attempt another cup of tea: before we get a chance to drink it we are sent to the General Hospital, which turns out to be a false alarm.

We arrive back at the station to see the divisional officer who is taking the exam waiting in the middle of the drill yard. I don't think that this is a good time to ask if we can have that cup of tea now.

Alfonce, the lad who is taking the exam, is German. He used to be in the German Army; he met his wife, who is an air stewardess, and moved to England. Sometimes when he is stressed or under pressure, he forgets himself and shouts orders in German, but I'm pleased to say that he comes through today's exams with flying colours.

Towards the end of his exam, my fire engine gets a call to stand by at Fordingbridge fire station. A pleasant twenty-minute drive, but still no cup of tea.

As soon as we arrive we put the kettle on and have our lunchtime cuppa at 4.30 pm.

Back to the station at 5.45, and home just after 6 o'clock. Eve goes shopping while I wash and tidy up. An hour's sit down, then off for my 30-minute sharp run. My legs ache, but I feel quite good and run at a good pace. As I'm running, I start to worry about pulling a muscle, or falling up on a kerb, and ruining everything for Sunday.

It's going to be quite a psychological battle up to Sunday, because it's constantly on my mind.

Day 4: Rest day

I'm riding in the back of the Water Tender Ladder today. The first priority this morning is to check the appliance; it spent the whole night at a large fire in Basingstoke. A make pumps 30, which is some major fire. On a fire of this magnitude, a great deal of equipment is used. Our job this morning is to check that all the equipment on the appliance belongs to us.

Our Water Tender is sent to Basingstoke as a relief crew, some 12 hours after the initial call. Apparently it was the largest fire in Hampshire for 17 years.

A morning spent checking and cleaning with no calls. I think that every fireman in Hampshire must have been to Basingstoke except us.

After lunch I spend the afternoon cooking, and making sandwiches ready for the youth quiz which is taking place at our station this evening.

The Water Tender arrives back from Basingstoke at 2.30 and the lads spend the rest of the afternoon cleaning and testing the equipment that was used.

Home just after 6 o'clock and, apart from driving Julie over to Bitterne, a quiet evening in front of the telly.

Day 5: A meander of a run for about 20 minutes

A morning of sorting out pensions, shopping and preparing a meal. I get a phone call from Julie asking if I can pick her up from college, as she is feeling unwell. She really does look unwell with a touch of flu, I think. I really hope that I don't catch it. I have a snack lunch, then off on my final run before the big day. I treat it as a slow jog, but even then my legs feel heavy. I'm sure it's all psychological.

Back home and a hot bath, then a bit of housework before getting ready for work. Eve arrives home at 4.15, so we have a chance to chat for an hour before I leave for work.

Driving the Hydraulic Platform tonight; straight after the parade I get a phone call from an ex-colleague and friend, Bob Blake, who now runs a pub in Scunthorpe, to wish me well for Sunday.

I remember when I did a 40-mile walk with Bob, he had blisters after 5 miles but kept going; he is 6ft 6in tall and was well known for sitting officers on his knee and giving them a kiss. Whether it was because of his size or what, but he used to get away with it.

After the checks, it's down to the local park for a game of football. I volunteer to go on radio watch. The last thing I need is a pulled muscle.

Eve brought the train tickets today: she will probably travel up on Sunday with her brother and his family. Kevin has to work and I don't think Julie is well enough.

I spend the drill period practising with the hydraulic platform, trying out various manoeuvres, and generally familiarising myself with the controls. Suppertime and no calls so far. The two pumps pick up a call at 11.30 to the General Hospital, which turns out to be a false alarm. Off to bed at midnight.

Day 6: Rest day

I look at my watch, it's 10 to 2 am, I can't sleep, what with Brian at the other end of the dormitory snoring so loudly, and the windows rattling. I also can't get the marathon out of my mind.

I get out of bed and make a cup of tea, and spend an hour reading my book, then back to bed and toss and turn until 7 am when we have to get up.

Breakfast and a general tidy-up: everyone wishes me well and I leave the station for home. I'm seeing Bob Donovan this morning at his home: he spends 45 minutes working to release the tension in my muscles, and teaching me how to use my muscles correctly. I leave feeling fit and raring to go.

Back home, and a bit of housework before spending a couple of hours at the allotment.

I cook the evening meal. Eve arrives home after 5 pm: she's off out this evening to a Pippa Dee party, so I spend the evening with Kev and Julie, and pack my bag ready for the off tomorrow.

CHAPTER 17

MARATHON WEEKEND

I say my farewells at home, and Eve drops me off at the railway station on time to catch the 10.15 train to Waterloo.

There are quite a few people on the station, and a few of these are obviously runners making the same trip as me. The train arrives on time, and I manage to find a seat: this must be a good start to the weekend.

A very relaxing journey of just over an hour, and we arrive on time at Waterloo. Lots of people in tracksuits, rushing here, there and everywhere. I decide to follow the crowds to Jubilee Gardens and the registration marquee.

I now notice, for the first time, the real hustle and bustle that I'm going to be part of for the next 30 hours or so. As I enter the marquee there are people everywhere queuing at various points. I look for the section displaying my race number, and join the queue. The atmosphere is great, laughing and joking, but I can also sense the nervousness of the unknown.

The chap in front of me tells me that he only told his wife that he was running last night. I sign in at the desk, and I'm given an envelope with more information. I make my way to the rail stand to collect my ticket to the start. Then off to another stand to collect my kitbag: you have to leave your kit in this bag at the start.

There are various trade stands offerings samples of drinks that are going to be available tomorrow. I also notice some people buying running shoes from a stand: I hope they don't need breaking in.

I make my way over to another stand to get my free ticket to the pasta party; this is being held at a hotel in Holborn.

It's then out into the fresh air, and a walk to Victoria to find my hotel. It's bitterly cold and raining. I make my way across Westminster Bridge, and notice all the barriers and grandstand being put into place.

The rain stops, and the snow starts. It was lovely in Southampton when I left.

I arrive in Victoria and try to find my hotel. There are a group of motorcycle police officers chatting, so I go and ask. Twenty minutes later after a very friendly chat about the Fire Service and the police, I'm pointed in the right direction, trying to remember all the places where they told me they would be tomorrow, so that I can give them a wave.

I arrive at my hotel about 1 o'clock and am shown to my basement room. It is clean and comfortable, but very small.

The first thing I like to do is to check the means of escape. I do this, and I now have two escape routes in my mind, should there be an emergency. The next thing is to locate the nearest toilet: luckily, it's right outside my room. The trouble is it's so small, I can barely sit down, one leg touching one wall, and the other leg touching the other. Anybody larger than me would have no chance.

I lay on the bed watching sport on TV; check the envelope that they gave me at registration: it contains my race number, which I pin onto my running vest straight away. Eve packed me four pins, which is lucky because I forgot to pick these up at registration.

The details tell me that I will be starting from the Red Start at Greenwich Park. There is also a note saying that it's best to get an early train to save rushing around before the start.

I decide to walk from my hotel to Waterloo East railway station, to check how long it takes. 20 minutes later, I arrive and now have the route in my head.

I return to my hotel, and rest and read for a couple of hours, before having a shower and change ready for the pasta party.

An announcement on the station states that there is a security incident at Holborn and therefore need to get off at Tottenham Court Road and walk.

I arrive at the hotel: the place is packed. The ticket entitles me to a meal and a drink. I join one of the queues and collect my meal. Very tasty, I even go back for seconds.

Various celebrities are being interviewed, and a video of last year's race is being shown. The camaraderie is brilliant, and everybody is now itching for tomorrow, and the start. Back to my hotel, and a very restless, nervous night.

Marathon Day

Well, it has arrived at last, after 16 weeks of training: aches, pains, blisters, but mostly great enjoyment and a sense of achievement.

I leap out of bed at 6 am, put the kettle on while I have a wash and shave. I have already planned my breakfast, 2 croissants with strawberry jam, and a couple of cups of tea. I brought the croissants from home with a small pot of jam.

Pack my bag, put on my running kit and tracksuit, minus my running shoes, which I like to put on just before the start. I wear an old pair of running shoes to the start, and then change.

I check out of the hotel, the proprietor wishes me good luck, and then set off on my planned route to Waterloo East railway station. The sun is shining and everything looks good for a great day. As I reach Westminster Bridge I notice it is closed off completely. The finishing line and famous clock are all in place, along with a grandstand for the VIPs.

I'm told that I can't use this bridge and must use another bridge some half a mile away along the Embankment. Everywhere is so quiet and peaceful. I have never seen London like this. I pass various homeless people sleeping under bridges or on benches as I make my way to the station. The number of people gradually increases until a large number of runners mix and joke together on Waterloo East station, waiting for the next of many trains that will carry 34,000 runners to the start of the race.

I manage to get a seat on the first train to arrive, the first thing that I notice is the very strong smell of liniment. Everyone is chatting, telling jokes, and giving advice during the 15-minute journey to Greenwich. We are then led by stewards for the 15-minute walk to the park where the famous start is.

We enter the park at 8 am; I decide to join the queue for the toilet. It takes some 20 minutes to reach the front. I make the most of this and rub Vaseline into all parts that come into contact with my shorts.

It's then up to one of the marquees giving away free tea and coffee, where I have a 5-minute sit-down with a cup of coffee. A chance to gather my thoughts; also to say a quiet prayer.

08.45 the gun fires to signify the start of the wheelchair

race which covers the same course as the runners.

9 am and we are asked to place our kitbags containing our tracksuits onto the lorries supplied. I look for the lorry with my number, and hand over my kitbag.

Thirty minutes to go: I start my warm-up and stretching. As I look around me there are people of all shapes and sizes going through similar routines.

9.20 I take my place at the starting line, behind the marker that includes my number. Everybody is anxiously looking at their watches and trying to stretch within the confines of the area, and wishing each other luck.

9.30 the gun fires to signify the start of the London Marathon. A large cheer goes up, a little jog of two steps, then everything comes to a sudden halt, followed by a slow walk. It takes nine minutes to reach the start line, that's when I start my watch.

It takes another couple of minutes before I start running. My hopes of a 9-minute mile are dashed, as it takes 11 minutes to reach the first-mile marker, purely because of the number of runners.

Things start to open up slightly now, as I try to settle into my normal running stride. There are crowds of people shouting and wishing us well. Someone from the crowd shouts out, "It's only another 25 miles, and it's all downhill!" He was right about the 25 miles.

I had already decided to take a drink at every other drink station for the first 13 miles, and then take it from there. After about 3 miles I feel comfortable and notice that I'm maintaining a 9-minute-mile pace.

The first major landmark is the Cutty Sark, which

is at the 6-mile mark. As we run around the famous ship, the crowds are marvellous, all shouting encouragement and various pieces of advice on how to get through the next 20 miles.

The drink stations are very well organised: you are offered various drinks, and I have decided that I will stick with SPAR water.

The next famous landmark is Tower Bridge, which is at the halfway mark. I'm still feeling good and maintaining the 9-minute-mile pace. Over Tower Bridge and past Bob Wilson, the ex-goalkeeper and commentator. He probably covers more miles then we do as he runs up and down interviewing people.

It's now onto the Isle of Dogs, which is a large loop starting at 16 miles and finishing on the 19-mile mark. It's very soul-destroying going over Tower Bridge: when you look down you can see the runners who are 10 miles in front of you, and coming out of the Tower of London.

Everywhere there are dance bands, Pearly Kings and Queens, young children holding out sweets and pieces of orange for the runners, and shouts of encouragement and support. I pass one of the tallest buildings in London at Canary Wharf, and head on to the Tower of London.

As I approach the Tower and those famous cobbles, I really begin to feel the strain. I now need to start fighting a mental battle in my mind. My body is telling me to stop, yet my mind is saying, "Don't you dare."

Past Bob Wilson once again, and onto the Embankment where I know Eve and Julie will be anxiously waiting for me to come through. I reach the 24-mile mark, but still haven't seen Eve and Julie. I begin to worry about them, and all sorts of things go through my mind. I plod on just looking for an excuse to stop running. Someone told me once, "A marathon is only 2 miles long, the last 2."

My legs really hurt; my mind is telling me to keep going. Along Birdcage Walk and the Parliament buildings come into view: I thought that this would really make me feel good.

No, it's a battle to keep going. The crowds are shouting and screaming to keep going, it is only the crowds who help me make it to and over the finishing line. I remember to stop my watch as I cross the finishing line.

The stewards guide and help me through the famous funnels where I'm presented with the medal, a foil blanket is placed around my shoulders. I feel really emotional at this stage as I walk along to the lorries carrying our bags.

I'm given fruit, bottles of SPAR water, also a carrier bag containing an assortment of gifts, which I decide to look at later. There are runners sitting, lying and limping around. I remember the training note about trying to keep moving, to avoid seizing up. A rather poorly looking chap is carried past me on a stretcher.

It's strange; I always thought that I would feel on top of the world at this point. But I don't: I feel totally dejected and exhausted. All I want to do is to find Eve and Julie and get right away from here.

I tell myself that I will never submit my body to this again, as I try to find the lorry with my bag. I eventually find the lorry, and really struggle to put my tracksuit on. Just lifting my feet to pull the trousers on is so hard; it takes me 3 or 4 attempts.

Off to Jubilee Gardens which is at the top of some steps. It feels like climbing Everest. I have to pull on the handrail and take one step at a time. Into the Gardens and off to locate the tree with the letter 'L' stuck to it where I'm meeting Eve and Julie.

What a good idea putting the letter of the alphabet on 26 different trees, you wait for your family under the one with your initial of your surname.

After 10-15 minutes Eve and Julie find me, and I feel really emotional as they both give me a cuddle and kiss and congratulate me on finishing.

Eve has rolls, crisps, chocolate and bottles of drink. I can't stop eating.

We now have the task of getting to Waterloo station, it's only about half a mile away, but it's up and down various bridges and stairs. My legs are so stiff I can hardly move.

We eventually arrive at Waterloo, only to find that our train is going to be diverted through Portsmouth and Fareham; this will put an extra hour on the journey.

We arrive home about 18.30. I decide to soak in a hot bath, lie there for about 40 minutes, dry off, and collapse in a heap on the settee.

After various phone calls from family and friends, I decide to open the goody bag that they gave me at the finish. The first thing that I pull out is a small sachet that says, "Add this to your first bath to help prevent stiffening." Oh well, I can always keep it for next year.

THE END

FIREMAN ON THE RUN